OUT OF DECEPTION

An Intense and Touching Story

Out of Deception
An Intense and Touching Story

e-mail: hopegraceandmercy@startmail.com
https://www.hopegraceandmercy.com

All scripture references are taken from the King James Version.

–Psalm 40:2–

He brought me up also **out of** an horrible pit, **out of the** miry **clay**, and set my feet upon a rock, and established my goings.

"A biography written to awaken and encourage many."

Edited by pastor Stephen Phillips – Freelife Church UK

This book is not written for the purpose of making money, but to help others who find themselves in a similar situation or who have loved ones in such a situation. The price of this book has been set to cover just the printing costs.

This book is lovingly dedicated to my sweet husband.

*My sweet Jan, we both have endured a lot, but our Father in Heaven
sees our heart through it all.
I know your desire is to follow God with all that is in you.
Your beautiful heart, your humbleness and
your love for God are treasures to me.
I pray every day for you with tears in my eyes,
I pray God keeps you safe.
The enemy has tried to steal, kill and destroy,
but God is much bigger.
Please come back home, and let us finish our race together.
I wait for you every day.
Much love, your wife Sabrina.*

The thief cometh not, but for to steal, and to kill, and to destroy:
I AM COME THAT THEY MIGHT HAVE LIFE,
AND THAT THEY MIGHT HAVE IT MORE ABUNDANTLY.
–John 10:10–

Table of Contents

Introduction

As a young child, I always had an awareness of God in my life, though I did not know Him. After a traumatic past in my childhood, I found my freedom in Jesus Christ. I am a born again Christian and have been since the end of summer 1992. I was baptized the following year.

19 years later my husband and I were lured into a deception, so much deeper than the one I experienced and escaped from in my childhood. In the fall of 2020, after a journey of nine hard years, God led me out of this wilderness. The Holy Spirit prompted me to write out the story of my life and thus this book was born.

Maybe you recognize yourself in my story but you are too ashamed or fearful to tell anyone. I want to encourage you to tell your story to your Heavenly Father who loves you, who knows and understands. Pray that He will give you someone you can trust. Confessing to others exposes the works of the darkness, and it opens the door to set you free. I pray this book may give you hope and courage.

1 Corinthians 10:11-13

Now all these things happened unto them for examples: and they are written for our admonition, upon whom the ends of the world are come. 12 Wherefore let him that thinketh he standeth take heed lest he fall. 13 There hath no temptation taken you but such as is common to man: but God is faithful, who will not suffer you to be tempted above that ye are able; but will with the temptation also make a way to escape, that ye may be able to bear it.

Preface

If you believe that Christians cannot be deceived, if you believe that Christians cannot be caught up into a cult, or perhaps you think this would never happen to you, then my story is for you. *I was deceived but I did not know I was deceived. I was part of a cult but I did not know I was part of a cult.*

This is my testimony, more a biography than a teaching. If you want to learn more about the main characteristics, tactics and marks of a false end-time ministry or even a religious cult, then I recommend that you also read my other book "WHY ARE YOU PERSECUTING ME?" written to be used as a ministry tool to help others.

I do not promote the things written in this book, so please do not seek after these things! On the contrary, you should run from these things as soon as you see them around you. If you recognize similar things happening in your life, please understand that you might be caught in a deception or even a cult.

The aim of this book is not to cast judgment, shame or embarrassment on anyone, but to help readers understand how people can be under the mind control and abuse of a narcissistic religious cult leader.

Romans 6:16
*Know ye not, that to whom ye yield yourselves servants to obey, **his servants ye are to whom ye obey**; whether of sin unto death, or of obedience unto righteousness?*

CHAPTER I: CHILDHOOD & YOUTH YEARS

EARLIER YEARS

No more love

"We cannot love you anymore as we used to do..." It felt like they ripped out my heart. I was just told that I had to break all soul-ties with my mother and someone else was going to be her soul-mate now. I felt broken, crushed and very confused. The realisation that I was not good enough anymore for her and that I was replaced, hurt me deeply. It also felt so final. The trust that my mother and I had in each other, our relationship, was broken in just a few seconds. And it was not even my own mother who told me this message.

The woman who told me this said this message was from God, and so I believed it and that made everything even harder. Because now I realized I was rejected not only by my mother, but also by God.

Our special times

"Has God spoken to you today?" This was one of the recurring questions my mother asked me when we had our special times together. For me it was special as I treasured these times, since they did not happen that much. Mostly, we went to a cheap place to eat something and then we had our talks about God. My mother was a strong believer in astrology. She read our horoscopes on a regular basis, and she was also sharing her knowledge about this subject with others. I did not always like "the others". In fact, I did not really like it at all that she was so involved in astrology.

I was only about 10 years old, a good child, just easy going and obedient to my mother. She had no problems with me at all, as far as I can remember. I did my best at school, although it seemed I had to do much more effort than the others in my class, to have good grades.

Moving

My mother and I were living in a small social rental apartment. My parents divorced when I was around three years old and so I lived mainly with my mother. Earlier years we lived in a nice big house with a beautiful garden. One day, when I was about seven years old, my uncle came to my school in the classroom and I had to go with him. The car was packed with our stuff and it was obvious we were moving. I did not know much of the detail, I only learned that the man whom my mother just left, was not nice to her.

We arrived at our new place, a big building with lots of small social apartments. Quiet a difference than the place we just left, with the nice big aquarium in the living room and my rabbit pets in the garden.

Every now and again I would visit my father for a weekend or during a school holiday. I really enjoyed going to my father. I loved him so much. In school when the teacher asked us about our parents and what their job was, I was always so proud to say my father worked in a lab in an electricity company. He lived in another town in a nice big house with a beautiful garden, where I could play with my friend next door. My father's wife was always very nice to me. We made a habit of watching television together in the kitchen, TV series like "Robin Hood", while enjoying some crisps or other good snacks. These were things I never did with my mother. In the social apartment things were much more serious and depressive. I remember the music my mother listened to, saddened me, just emotional melancholic music. She was very

14

unhappy and many times she sought her comfort in alcohol.

I asked her if she wouldn't mind if I went to live with my father now. She said it was ok. I was still so young, just a tiny little girl, but I left the apartment with anxiety in my heart about my poor mother who was now all by herself in her unhappy state.

Ignored

My father also turned to drink at times and that made me very unhappy. I wanted more of his attention and therefore I went with him to the local football club, only to find that I was totally ignored in a company of men who were drunk. I loved horses and begged him to go with me to a place where I could ride a horse. I remember he did once and one day he gave me a big poster of a horse. On another occasion he was drunk and I did not feel comfortable in the way he was acting, so I asked him to please take me back to my mother. He drove me back in the car.

No not him!

I was back in the big building with the many social apartments. It looked like a huge prison to me. I never liked it nor felt comfortable in that place. The door of the apartment opened and I looked straight at the eyes of a strange man sitting on the couch. I was only about 9 years old but I knew immediately what was going on. My first thoughts were "No not you! Please mother not him!" I had never seen this man before, but I did not like him at all. And he did not like me. It was as if we could read each other's mind. I heard the voice of my mother who said "Oh this man missed his bus so he stayed the night". Grief and sadness filled my heart. What could I do or say? I said nothing and just accepted the situation. But deep down I knew I would have to watch over my mother now to protect her from this strange man, who just took advantage of her.

My new stepfather

They married and the strange man moved into our little apartment. He was a nervous man and had this awful habit of clicking his fingers in a particular way, which made a certain noise. He did this mostly when he was lying down on the couch. Whenever I heard his fingers click, I knew trouble was coming. It was as if he was building up anger inside of him, and waiting for my mother so he could let it out on her. She was working full time in an electronics company. Every day she took the bus back and forth. He was doing some business in making and selling comic greeting cards. After he married my mother, she found out that he had a lot of debt.

Abused

I was downstairs in the cellar where everyone had a little storage place. It looked like prison cells to me. I was always a bit scared down there by myself. I was playing with my doll. A man approached me and told me I had to touch him. I didn't want to, but could not escape. I quickly did it and then ran upstairs. I told my mother and a little later I had to go with her to the police office to identify the man. I recognized him. He never knew I was there at the police station.

Ironically enough, something similar happened only a few weeks later. I was visiting my father and playing in the garden. A man stopped at the street and asked me if I could go with him and show him the way to a certain place. Very naïve as I was as a little girl, I went with him to the corner of the next street, and there he threw me in the grass and wanted to abuse me. I started to scream and was able to escape from his grip and ran back home. Many years later, when I became a Christian, I understood the enemy wanted to destroy my life during my childhood.

Blue eye

This is how they called my mother in the environment where we lived, blue eye. It still hurts me today when I think about it. The man she married used to beat her regularly for no reason. I noticed that when his eyes changed, his behaviour changed in seconds. I knew he was taken over by evil spirits during those times. One time he took glasses and jars and just threw them over the balcony. He was out of himself and did not think there could be people downstairs on the street.

One day his demonic possession was acting up and he was sitting in my bedroom. I was about 10 years old and had just come home from school and wondered why he was in my room. He was trying out all the different markers on my little desk. I gently asked him to leave. Then he looked at me, stood up, took the horse picture from the wall and tore it in pieces before my eyes. I cried out to him in anger because this poster with the horse was the only thing my father ever gave me, and I loved it. I had it for several years.

I ran to the door trying to escape the apartment, but he stopped me. I was terrified. Then he told me that he would beat me into my grave. But he never touched me.

Let go of her!

My mother continued to receive beatings from him. He hit her on her back with the wooden chairs from the dining room. One day he strangled her, I went into the kitchen, took a knife and told him if he didn't let go of her, I would kill him. I was still only about 10 years old. This is how children get into jail and special institutions for bad behaviour, but luckily not for me as he let go of her.

After that he used to lock the door that separated my bedroom with the living room. As I was lying in my bed, I heard the noise of his hands that hit her. He was yelling at me "What are you going to do now to help her?" Tears streaming down my face as there was nothing I could do to help my poor mother. I hated that man with all that was within me.

Chains

During that same period, I had a very terrifying experience. Next to my bed I saw the devil and he was binding me with iron chains. Was this the result of my mother's astrology and her laying hands on people? I knew she was getting deeper and deeper into things that were strange and scary to me. I heard weird things from her that I never heard from other people. But why was I a victim? I was reading books at those times called "The black stallion". It was about a race horse. One of the foals bred from the black stallion was called "satan" in the books. I was always very troubled when I read this name, and thought "why does it have to be this name for a horse?" I wondered if the books were still good for me to read. I always enjoyed reading them as it was a way for me to escape reality for a moment.

Derby

I could not wait for school holiday to begin, get in the car and go to the sea. My aunt had an apartment there and when I was 10 years old, she took me with her. Very soon I discovered a riding school Derby, very close to our apartment. I just had to walk through the dunes, and there were the horses! This was paradise on earth for me. Every day I went horse riding. After a few holiday's over there I basically lived in the riding school and was allowed to make walks with the horses on the beach. I took care of horses from owners and could ride them for free. I had my friends there, we had our bedrooms in the riding school and we basically took control over the horses and everything about them. This was such a different life than the one I had at home. But every day I was worrying about my mother hoping she would be doing ok and not suffering too much. I was happy at the sea with my aunt and the horses but felt guilty for leaving my mother behind.

Watchdog

My mother and her husband were both drinking a lot. My mother went to cafes and pubs to drink alcohol. Then when she was drunk, she would be teaching the people around her about astrology and laying hands on people to heal them. I was her "watchdog" and kept the men away from her when they came too close. I also watched her purse, so they would not steal anything. I could not do this all the time, but whenever I could, I was around. I was hoping she would just stop drinking and come home. It was a terrible time, it felt like hell. Sometimes when it was too late at night, I had to leave my mother behind in the pub, take the bus and get back home. This went on for several years.

I tried to focus at school, but it was very hard. The other classmates started bullying and excluding me, as they saw I was not doing the "normal stuff" like they did, going out at the weekends, having boyfriends, drinking and smoking etc. I never touched alcohol or cigarettes or any drugs. I had one friend who was nice enough to walk next to me during the breaks between classes at school.

Another riding school

I was able to go to other riding schools, and sometimes my mother went with me. She was not interested in my riding lessons, but this was another opportunity for her to also escape the home situation. Unfortunately she always got drunk in the bar and was talking to others about her horoscopes, astrology and other related things. I felt so ashamed and wished she would not come with me anymore, where my friends from the riding school could see her in this state.

She was meeting other people interested in the paranormal and I felt very uncomfortable and knew things were not right. When I was with her, I waited in another room until she was ready to go back home. The smell of alcohol filled the car. It was a miracle we never had an accident when the car was moving from one side to the other in the late night hours.

Blanca

Blanca was waiting for me. Every morning before I went to school, I stopped at the field to give him my apple. He was such a sweet big horse. One day I met the owner and he told me that I could ride his horse. With my riding saddle on the handlebars of my bike, I was riding through the streets on my way to the field. This was a different life for me and I was so very thankful I could do this for free.

The debt-collector

The debt-collector came to our apartment on odd occasions. He just opened all the drawers and took what he liked, things that had any value. I was so sad for my mother who lost her special things due to the debts of the man she married. She did not have much; most of her furniture was pretty old. So she treasured the little things she kept in her drawers, like some old coins. I felt so sorry for her and could not understand why that debt-collector had no compassion. I heard my mother say that according to the law he had to leave us a bed and a chair. But the man did not take the furniture at this time.

THE NEIGHBOURS

Flee the apartment

"He is back!!" I panicked when I looked through the window and saw the car from my stepfather. It was actually my mother's car but he used it. We were packing to move out. He came in the apartment and I pretended I was cleaning out the cabinets. He saw something was off, so he decided to stay and not go back to work anymore. The moving company could come at any minute now and we still had to pack so many things. Finally, he decided to go back to work anyway and I waited until I could not see his car anymore. Then we quickly packed everything in the few boxes we had. The moving company was here and they were surprised we were not ready. They helped us pack and we were out quite soon. I was about 14 years old then and it was one of the scariest days of my life.

I was so relieved when we could lock the house and be finally safe inside, away from him. My mother found this rental house and it was really nice. Quiet big compared to the apartment we lived in for so many years. I had a nice room upstairs and we had a big garage and a garden! We lost the car but that was the least of our worries.

Not again...

"What shall I destroy first?" he said. He managed to force the door with a pair of scissors and came in. It was like a horror movie. I thought he would destroy it all, but for some reason he did not do it and left. He waited for my mother on the street when she was walking to her bus stop to get to work. He was violent again in the middle of the street. It seemed that even the police did not care as they just passed by and did not do anything. How much longer before we would be out of this nightmare? He finally calmed down after a while and we did not see him again.

White or black magic?

My mother told me to look up the meaning of my dreams in a special book she had. She got deeper into the paranormal and continued to practise her magnetization, by passing on her energy to people through the laying on of her hands. Thus they would be physically healed. Also automatic writing was part of her learning process, where she sought connection with her spirit guides.

She was also seeing a clairvoyant and learned how to use tarot cards and how to read the palm lines on people's hands. I didn't feel comfortable with all this, but I believed my mother was a good woman and that she was doing all this with good intentions trying to help others.

The penetrating smell of the incense sticks filled the whole house. I was always hoping my mother would forget to light the sticks as they brought such a strange atmosphere in the house that I did not like.

When the topic was brought up, I tried to convince people around us, that I knew, that my mother was doing the right thing, namely the white magic. I could not handle it when someone would speak a bad word about her, not after all the suffering she went through. In fact, I did everything to defend and promote her. I was still her watchdog. She was also teaching me to look at someone's nose. When the shape of the nose was sharp the people were mean and sharp. When the nose was formed thicker, the people were nice and soft.

Disappointed

But deep inside of me, I was disappointed that my mother was not just like other mothers. There was no happiness in the house, we never laughed, we never did anything funny and everything in her life was surrounded with the paranormal. This was the only thing she was talking about with other people. Besides that, she still sought contact with others who were involved in the same paranormal activity, and I did not like these people, as it all seemed so dark and mysterious to me and away from reality.

The neighbours

Oh finally! Contact with normalcy. Our neighbours were a precious beautiful family. They were so very nice to me, as they had compassion for me after they learned everything we went through. Very soon we became close and most of the time we were eating our meals together in their house. They were Catholics and so we all went to the Church together on Sundays, as one happy family. However I was not happy. I felt very uncomfortable around people, including our neighbours. They were all so spontaneous, laughing with each other and I wondered how I could be like them. For me, spontaneity was not a gift. I did my very best, but it must have been obvious for the others that I struggled to break through the wall around me. My mind was also confused in many ways, so I was just quiet most of the time.

No more love

"We cannot love you anymore as we used to do…" Those were the hardest and most hurtful words I had ever heard. She said the message came from God. God? How could God decide such a thing? She also said that she and my mother were now soul-mates and I could not stand in the way. My whole world fell apart at that moment. Then she left via the backdoor. I was nailed to the ground, paralyzed. Did I do something wrong? Was it because I was not spontaneous enough as they were?

Immediately I was filled with guilt truly believing this decision from God was my own fault.

Here was I, a young teenager between 15 and 16 years old, with no mother and no father. I hadn't seen my father for many years. I did my very best at school and managed to get through all my years. My class mates were treating me now with some more respect, as we were all getting a bit older. But no one knew what was going on at home. I never had friends over to visit, simply because I had no friends at school. And anyway, I wanted to avoid contact between anyone I knew and my mother, just in case she would start to talk about her art of divination. Because I knew people would not understand and it also made me feel ashamed.

The fireplace sessions

"You have one month to change!!" shouted the voice out of my mother's mouth during a séance. It was one of the spirits who took control over my mother when she functioned as a medium. She was in a trance and her spirit was somewhere between heaven and earth. These séances were terrifying for me, as the spirits did not seem to like me. They shouted how bad I was and I did not understand why I was a target for them, because I did everything in my power to be a good daughter. The spirits told us that we were a special privileged family, as these spirits normally don't come to households. But these spirits were shouting at me and I felt so scared at those times. My mother always knew who was talking through her vessel. I believed these spirits could read my thoughts and thus I felt watched and observed all the time.

Answers and guidance were also sought by spirits via other means. Things had changed drastically since that moment the neighbour told me they could not love me anymore as they used to do. There was no trace of spontaneity left in me now, and every time I was around my mother and the neighbours, I tried very hard to act "normal", hoping they would accept me again. But I was in so much stress and fear. Fear to lose my mother forever. I was traded in for the neighbours.

Help me!

"Help me!" I woke up and heard my mother shouting from her bedroom. Evil spirits were attacking her. I walked into her bedroom and slept the rest of the night next to her. Now she had peace again. Most nights the neighbour woman slept next to her, and then there were no attacks. Her husband and children stayed at home. I wondered if they were ok with that, but I was afraid to ask any questions.

With everything going on, so much tension had built up between me and the neighbours, especially with the woman, and so I had to stay in our house for most of the time. In the morning, my mother came downstairs with the neighbour woman. My "hello" probably sounded very forced. They hardly talked to me anymore. They left the house via the backdoor and disappeared through an opening in the garden to the neighbours place. I was so sad and lonely.

My mother gave me 100 Belgium francs per week to buy my food. This is equal to 3 dollars per week. She continued to have her meals with the neighbours in their house. During Christmas time they brought me a plate with food, while everyone else was celebrating together next door.

Hell is back

Strange things were happening also in our house that scared me. I felt like hell was back in my life again. Sometimes I wondered if the life we had with the man who was beating her, was better than this one. My mother was still drinking, but not as much as she used to do in the past while she was still living with that man.

The monastery

People were nice here and the atmosphere was so different. I was sent here by my mother and the neighbours in this Catholic building to spend a few weeks to change myself into a spontaneous happy person. I did not feel judged or observed all the time, though I was very uncomfortable in the group. We were all sitting in a big circle. Everyone was sharing something about their life. Now it was my turn. My heart was racing inside of me when I heard myself talking about the things happening at home. There was silence and eyes filled with compassion, were staring at me. I did not plan to do this I guess it came just spontaneously?

The experience of having people around me who were so touched in unbelief about my story, broke the wall around me. This was the first time that I was sharing my story with others. These people were telling me all that was happening at home was not ok. Actually I loved their response. I felt such a relief and was in peace for the first time in a very long time. Was this God's doing? Or had I just made a terrible mistake, I wondered, while doubt mixed with my newly won peace.

"Hello!" With a smile on my face I went to my mother and the neighbours who were picking me up and observing every move I made. Did I pass my test? Was I changed now into the being that they expected? Not really, back at home the tension was back right away and things went on as before. I was so disappointed in myself.

Reincarnation

My mother told me that this was her last life on earth and now she was ready to meet God. I, on the other hand, still had many lives on earth before I would be ready to see God. Just the thought that God and I would be separated for such a long time, made me very discouraged. All comments and observations towards me were negative and the value I had about myself was as good as zero. I still looked up my dreams in that book because my mother told me to do so. I was going through the pages, looking up every single detail connected with my dreams, hoping to find one positive comment. But mostly there was nothing encouraging in the explanation. As for my mother, her dreams were explained as very good and hopeful.

Not good enough

I tried my very best to please my mother and the neighbours. I cleaned the house and did the dishes. I never complained nor rebelled. While being alone in the house, I played the melancholic music from my mother. I was just filled with so much grief and depression took a hold on me.

A dream comes through

The phone rang and it was for me. Could it be true? Was it really him? "You can come to my place to work with the horses. My sister will pick you up at the train station." I couldn't have been more happy and excited! I was going to work with the horses from a famous national rider that I really liked. At one of his competitions I had gathered all my courage and walked up to him, asking him if I could come to help him.

I drew a picture of one of his best breeding stallions to give to him. "Do you want to have some tea?" I don't know how long I was stirring in the tea pot that I prepared for him before he came in the kitchen, repeating that question over and over in my head. I slept in his sister's room. The family house was filled with photographs of horses. There were lots of horse stables. I could work out one of his horses. I better get rid of my shame and uncertainty and quickly, I said to myself, if I wanted to impress him. He was older than me and he looked very mature and all grown up.

"This is very beautiful, you even covered his weak point!" he said when I handed him the picture that I drew. I worked very diligently on that and made sure it was an exact copy of the real photo that I had from that horse.

A thousand emotions went through this 17 year old girl when I was sitting next to him in the big truck. He was driving to a training ground to work out one of his horses. Later we went to a competition. He was riding that black breeding stallion from the picture I drew. It took a good hand to control breeding stallions in the middle of many other horses. But he had a very gentle hand and handled his horses with much respect. That is what I liked about him so much. He shouted at his groom, he was angry at her, and I was a bit shocked by his reaction, she was doing something wrong and according to his response, it didn't seem to be the first time that he had to correct her.

He told me to get on the breeding stallion and to warm him up in the arena. Now my heart stood still. Here I was, sitting on one of the most famous breeding stallions in the middle of other horses with their best riders. I had no experience at all riding a stallion like this. He will probably buck me off, or attack another horse, I was thinking. The horse was walking calmly. He seemed to respect me and not take advantage of my inexperience and fear. Horses were galloping all around me and jumping over the obstacles to warm up.

"Finally he is coming!" I got off the horse and he got on. He seemed to approve how I handled him, gentle and nice. This was a moment I would never forget.

A possible marriage?

The yearly vacation was planned for my mother, the neighbours and their two daughters. The caravan was all ready to go. But I could never be part of their trips. Gladly I could go back to work with the horses from the national rider. My mother told me I was going to marry him and I would have a stable full with horses. Oh this was the best news ever! I felt I was healed instantly.

This time I stayed at his groom's small apartment, who was on vacation. This apartment was on the property of a business man and the stables were here also. The national rider came here daily to train the horses. My job was to clean out the stables, feed the horses and give them exercise. I was allowed to ride some of them, which was really great. I was still so uncertain on the inside, but tried to hide it any possible way. Was this truly the man I was going to marry? He had no idea about my wild dreams, though he was very nice to me.

Scattered dreams

"You are not going to marry him!" The voice of my mother sounded very merciless and she made it appear that I had been punished by God and now this blessing of marrying the man with the horses was taken away. As happy and excited as I had been before, now I was so unhappy and depressed again. What had I done wrong? I really did not know, as no further explanation was given to me. And I was not allowed to see him anymore. Later my mother told me I was going to marry someone else I knew from the horse-world. But this did not come to pass either.

Suicide

On my way back from the riding school, I planned to stay in the woods and just sit there until I died. I figured this must have been the easiest way where no one would find me. But I always went back home. However, suicide was filling my thoughts. Many times I just crossed the busy highway without looking. Often it is only when we are getting older that we realize how God protected us so many times in the past.

Nevertheless I continued to love the horses and always found a way to ride them for free. At least with the horse people I had some friends and in the stables no one was condemning me, watching me or rebuking me. This was a wonderful way for me to escape the house and just survive. But I still did not talk to anyone about my situation.

No more contact

There was a nice couple living close by and my friend and I could ride their horses. The lady gave us a big ice cream and I loved to sit in their jeep on the way to the horses. One day my mother told me I could not have any contact with that couple anymore, as the man had bad thoughts about me. What? I never noticed anything of that. He and his wife were mostly together and he did not give me any special attention. But I obeyed my mother, as she heard this from "above".

Headache and migraines

When I was around 18 years old, I got daily very strong headaches and terrible migraines. It felt like a band tightened very strong around my head. Today 32 years later, I still feel the band around my head and suffer migraines from time to time, but not so frequently anymore as in the past. However my head has never been able to relax, not even for one moment, since that time when I got headaches.

God and nature

In all this, I loved to go out in nature and talk with God. I always believed there was a God in Heaven who cared for us. I just didn't know Him very well. One day on one of my walks, I was crying out to God. Suddenly the sun was shining through the trees on me. Some moments in our life are special and precious and this was such a moment. I just knew God had heard me and the sun was warming my face and heart.

A job

I finished school and my mother told me I had to go to work now. I found a job in a supermarket. I also did some other jobs in between to earn some extra money. I made it a habit to look out for nice but quite expensive gifts that my mother would like, to give her on special days. Despite the fact I hardly got any attention, I still loved her and wanted to bless her.

My grandmother

She was not my real grandmother, but in my heart she was. She was just an elderly lady that my mother knew. One day, I decided to go visit her all by myself. She was a Christian lady and told me about God and the Bible. I truly loved this lady and I started to pour out my heart to her. For the first time since I opened up to the people in the Catholic building, I now opened my heart totally to this sweet old lady. Every time I visited her, she was asking me how I was doing and she was a very good listener. I did not tell my mother that I was telling this elderly lady everything that was going on in our house. And apparently she didn't know.

I was always waiting to be rebuked by those spirits who spoke through the mouth of my mother, as for sure they must have known what I was doing! But no rebuke came, not for this. Could it be that these spirits did not know everything after all? I started to wonder and it gave me even more boldness when I visited the elderly lady.

That is not from God

"It is not ok what is happening in that house" she said to me many times. "That is not from God". I felt the same relief coming over me when I heard those words, as when I was in the Catholic building. I was so hoping she was right. At least here with my grandmother I found some rest and peace. She was always prepared to listen to me. She never condemned nor judged me and one day I entrusted her with my confessions of some very sad and bad things I had experienced. Men had taken advantage of me in my search for love and acceptance. She told me God had forgiven me and it was ok. Really? Wow, that was great to hear. I loved God, but it was hard for me to believe that He loved me too. Since I believed all the hardship I went through, was put on me by God to punish me, because I was not good enough.

I miss him

I missed my father so much. I always longed to have a good relationship with him, but that did not really work out very well. He never showed much interest in me. I had not seen him for many years. My mother said it was better for me not to see him.

My diary

I spent all my free time with the horses and in the riding school with my friends. It was my escape from reality. The stress level became so high, and I started to write down my emotions in a diary. It was just a cheap writing book. My book became my new friend and I wrote down everything I struggled with, even with the neighbours. One day when I came in my room upstairs, my diary friend was exposed and had been read by the neighbours and my mother. They broke my trust and I felt angry, ashamed and betrayed. Could I not really have any form of privacy? Now they knew everything about me and how much I struggled in all my thoughts and emotions about them.

Sunday's

Sunday's were stressful days for me. It was time to go to church but how could I avoid the neighbours and my mother? I did not know how to behave anymore when I saw them. I was hopeless at being spontaneous, so I tried to avoid them as much as possible. I made sure I was sitting a few rows behind them, so they could not watch me. Then I rushed home to make sure I made it back before them.

The priest

The priest was a friend of the neighbours. Sometimes he visited them. He was a very nice humble man and a desire grew in me to speak to him about the situation. But how would he react? After all, these were his friends. The door opened and he invited me in. With a trembling heart I told him what was really happening in our house for all those years. He said this was not ok and he told me I had to leave the house. Leave the house? But how, where do I go?

A prayer of despair

I could not handle the stress anymore. Sometimes I went to the Catholic Church to pray. I asked the Saints to help me. Now I was in my bedroom upstairs and I cried out to God and all the Saints I knew in pure despair. I told Him I could not take it anymore and would jump out of the window to kill myself.

The thought came to me to call my father. Wow, I was so nervous! I dialled the number and my grandmother, the elderly lady, picked up the phone. I recognized her voice right away.

Now I was very confused. She told me I must have dialled the wrong number. I tried again and now I saw that my father's number was almost the same. This time my father's wife picked up the phone.

He looks so old

I opened the door and there stood an old looking man. He was not that old, only in his forties. But when you have not seen people for so many years, they look old at first sight. It was weird to see my father again. He came into the house and we talked a little bit. I did not tell him anything about the situation with my mother or the neighbours. Then he just said if I ever wanted to move out and go live by myself, he would help me and make amends for all the years he had not taken care of me. I was speechless but jumping within me for joy, because I knew this was a direct answer to my prayer of despair! Wow, was God really on my side after all?

My first beating

"How could you have done that!" she shouted. I buried my face in my hands as I felt her fists on my head. This was as much as I could remember; the very first time my mother ever hit me. She was angry because I just told her I went to the bank to take away her power of attorney over my account. There was no money in my account. She always had free access to use anything she needed from what I earned at my work place. I was shocked and hurt at the same time, because she seemed only concerned about my money she would not have access to anymore.

MOVING OUT

Moving day

The horse van arrived at the door and we could start loading my stuff. These were friends I knew from the stables. "Bye" I said to my mother, hoping to receive a word or perhaps a goodbye hug? She just looked at me and then closed the door. A whole new adventure was now in front of me. I was able to stay at my friend's place for a while until I could move into my apartment. She was very nice and I knew her for several years.

My new place

My father kept his word and bought me everything I needed. Here I was, 20 years old now and in my first rental apartment, pretty small but big enough for me. In the first months I was really struggling financially, because I did not have anything to start with and rent and deposit had to be paid. I was determined to get through my debt as quick as possible and I spent as little as I could on food. I told the bank I would be able to pay off my debt.

Healing

Whenever I went outside, I was looking around and hoping I would not see my ex-neighbours as I did not know how to behave in their presence. Whenever I was still in the house, my mother taught me to do a certain ritual every day to protect myself. Would God be angry at me if I didn't do it today? I will skip one day and see what happens. I soon learned that nothing bad was happening to me and I renounced these daily rituals. The freedom I had was wonderful. But it took a while before I could actually fully enjoy my freedom, as I had to be healed and be set free of so many things from the past.

Also physically I was not doing so well. My back was giving me lots of pain and I had to see a manual therapist regularly.

My aunt

"Your aunt dropped these off for you". The bags were filled

with towels and other things I could use well. I missed my aunt. The times at sea with the horses were still the best memories of my life, but I hadn't seen my aunt for many years. Before we moved to the house, my mother told me I could not see my aunt anymore. She said she was involved in dark occult things. That surprised me, as I never noticed anything of that when I was with her. But I obeyed my mother and so all contact was broken. Now I was in a dilemma, could I keep the nice gifts she just gave me? I was afraid that the things she gave me were infected with her dark occult magic, and could influence me badly, so I decided to throw it all away. It was a hard thing to do, as I really liked the things and could use them.

She opened the door and it was a bit weird to see her again. She too looked older after so many years. I learned that she sold the apartment at sea. I was sad to hear that, but I was too old now anyways for riding school "Derby" and spending the nights there with my friends among the horses. My aunt was not so happy because I had not visited her for so many years. I explained that my mother forbade me to contact her because she was involved in dark occultist matters. My aunt was so surprised to hear this and said she had never been involved in such things. I believed her. Now I regretted that I threw away all the things she gave me before.

Go back to the house?

I was struggling again and could not pay my rent. I prayed and told God I had to go back to my mother's house if I had no money. I was confused and hurt. Shortly afterwards a cheque came in the mail. It was from my aunt and it was just enough to cover my rent for that month. Oh wow God really answered my prayer and so quickly! I was so happy that I could stay in my little apartment.

A new job

I was doing a bit better financially and I decided to quit my job and follow an additional training course for business administration, which I ended successfully in April 1992. I still received an income while studying, so that was really great. I found a new job in a place where I had to help abused women and children.

The place was run by Catholic nuns. Most of the women were abused by their husband, so they stayed there in the house for shelter and safety. This for me was not an easy job as I was confronted again with violent men. But it gave me an income and free meals at work.

This will be your husband

Summer time 1992. I still visited my grandmother. She always gave me something to eat for that week. I also received a big wooden crucifix that I hung in my bedroom. I really liked that.

"He is really nice and someone for you." She repeatedly spoke these words to me about a young man who was part of the Evangelical church she attended. I told her I was not interested in any man. Then she invited me to the barbecue of that church. It was a beautiful day and many people were there that I did not know.

"This will be your husband". I heard this voice very clearly speaking to me. There was no one near me that was talking to me, but I knew instantly this was God speaking to me. I thought "Ok". I agreed and accepted it just like that. I observed the young man carefully and asked my grandmother who he was. She said this was the young man she had talked about to me. Oh wow, this was truly amazing! The young man never got out of my sight anymore for the rest of that day and for the next three years.

CHAPTER II: JESUS SAVES!

BORN AGAIN

1993 – Born again and baptized

June 27, 1993. I was standing in front of the Church reading my testimony. I was so nervous but got through my speech. I heard the good news in this Church almost 9 months ago, that Jesus Christ had come to earth to give me eternal life. He died on the cross for my sins, He paid the full price and He was risen and alive.

When I heard that, I realized what my mother told me about reincarnation was not the truth. I did not have to live several lives in order to become good enough to eventually meet God. God was here in my heart and every day I could meet Him! I only had to be born again once, but in a spiritual way! This was the best news ever for me and it brought me so much joy and also huge relief.

Today was the day I had been waiting for. I was going to be baptized:

"Know ye not, that so many of us as were baptized into Jesus Christ were baptized into his death? Therefore we are buried with him by baptism into death: that like as Christ was raised up from the dead by the glory of the Father, even so we also should walk in newness of life." Romans 6:3-4

I received a certificate that said:
"I am crucified with Christ: nevertheless I live; yet not I, but Christ liveth in me: and the life which I now live in the flesh I live by the faith of the Son of God, who loved me, and gave himself for me." Galatians 2:20

Christ was captured in my heart and I was so thankful for His forgiveness for my past. This was such a different life. I met other brothers and sisters in Christ and most importantly, I had my little Bible that I was reading and studying. I also learned the things my mother was doing and all that she taught me was not God's hand, but the enemy's. I now knew that satan had tried to destroy my life. But God saved me, hallelujah!!

Confrontation

"Hi, I would like to give you this; it is about God and…" She abruptly interrupted me and said she had broken all contact with my mother and she wanted nothing more to do with all this. Her face turned all red when she walked away and disappeared in the crowd. "But this is different." I still wanted to tell her. It was a very unexpected meeting and I just wanted to give her the leaflet I had in my hands about Jesus Christ and His work of salvation for all of us. Wow, I was shocked, my mother and the neighbours apparently had broken all contact.

Wedding invitation

"I cannot buy a gift, I don't have the money" she said. There was no joy in her blue-grey eyes. She looked so unhappy. My future husband and I were looking at my mother and told her that it was ok she did not need to buy a gift for us. We were just here to introduce my fiancé and invite her to the wedding. I felt sorry for my mother, as she was still so deep in the deception. The atmosphere was so different here in her house, it was hard for me to be here. So many memories came back. But I was happy to learn that she had an elderly friend who was a blessing for her.

Fired

For a while, I was evangelizing at work whenever I had the opportunity. In my free time, my little red car was filled with people from the refuge. Sometimes we drove to the beach and the ones who were willing, came with me to the church for Bible study. The nuns told me I was not allowed to do this anymore. But how could all these people be helped without hearing the Word of God? Jesus was my salvation, so they needed Him too. I had a nice private talk with the head nun, and I told her if I could not tell the people here about Jesus, then I could not work here any longer.

"Wow, I have never met such a young person as you with so much faith!" she said, with a big smile on her face and really impressed. If I resigned, I would have no income, so the nun told me she would fire me. This way I had an income until I found another job. That was really nice of her and I saw God's providing hand in this. Now I had more time to plan my wedding!

MARRIED

July 8, 1995 – Wedding day!

"Wow you are so beautiful…" Those are the words every bride wants to hear on her wedding day. Today was finally the day for us. My grandmother, the elderly lady, had it right after all about this young man. I could not be happier. I was ignoring the pain in my head that had been there for the last 7 years. It was a beautiful day. We found a rental house surrounded with fields, quite old, but we liked it, as it had lots of space. My husband and I were involved in charity work, so our house was perfect as we needed this extra space. The property also had some stables that were occupied with cows from the landlord next door. I loved to watch the cows when they were grazing so close to our house. It would be nice to have a horse here.

Attacks

We spent our honeymoon in Greece. The first night however I was attacked by a demonic presence. Little did we know that we were up for a serious battle for the next three years. I already had counselling sessions before we were married, to receive my deliverance from all the demonic experiences in the past.

The attacks were really severe. I was manifesting strongly during the nights and was stretching and forcing my body in certain directions to the extreme. I could not help myself. Evil forces took control over my body. As a result, my back was hurt and damaged even more. My husband and I did not get a lot of sleep during those first three years of our marriage. It was as if the devil was not happy that my husband and I were married and he tried to destroy us.

1997 – Invalid

My physical pain got worse. I successfully finished another course for business administration and received a recommendation letter in February 1996, after a month internship work in a hospital. However, I had to leave that work place several times, as I couldn't bear the pain in my head and back. The lack of sleep, stress and pain took its toll. I stopped looking for a job and had manual therapy and many examinations to find out what was wrong in my body.

After seeing several specialists and undergoing many tests in hospitals, I was declared an invalid on May 20, 1997. The years after only got worse and I had pain in my whole body, in every muscle and vertebrae. Tendon infections, spasms and a pinched nerve were occurring on top of the other pains. The headaches and migraine attacks were constant. I knew and understood all this physical suffering was a consequence of all the trauma and hurt of the past.

Hell is back...

The demonic attacks were still there. Whenever my husband left for work, I was tortured with thoughts of suicide. Why was I not allowed to have any peace, neither spiritually nor physically?

In all this I continued to love God and kept my faith. I told the doctors that God would heal me. My husband was really wonderful and supported me as good as he could. He was working fulltime. During the nightly attacks, he always quoted scriptures and did warfare against those demons manifesting through me:

"Because he hath set his love upon me, therefore will I deliver him: I will set him on high, because he hath known my name. He shall call upon me, and I will answer him: I will be with him in trouble; I will deliver him, and honour him. With long life will I satisfy him, and shew him my salvation."
Psalm 91:14-16

The voices and visions are gone!

After three years of ongoing prayers for my deliverance, I finally received rest in my head. One morning the demonic voices and visions were gone and they never returned. Oh hallelujah, all praises to God! I was so very thankful for those two brothers in Christ who faithfully prayed with me and my husband during all those years. It had not been easy, but God was the One who gave us the strength and courage to persevere during those years.

The nights were also becoming "normal" now that the attacks were gone, and we could enjoy more sleep. I was determined I would never be part of any occultists practises ever again.

Suffering

However my physical suffering continued on. The pain in my back and neck was so severe. I saw many therapists who tried to help me by manipulating my muscles and vertebrae. Sometimes it felt as if they were breaking my vertebrae. Every session was so painful but I never had any relief. One specialist even suggested an operation to fix my scoliosis, but I refused. Medication had no positive effect on me, besides the fact that it made me sick, so I did not take any painkillers. I strongly believed that God was going to heal me supernaturally and I didn't want to see any more doctors.

My horse

I still sought my comfort and distraction in horses. Around 1998 I had the desire and opportunity to buy a horse. He was young and a very beautiful quality horse, coming from a good bloodline. My husband was not fond of the idea to have a horse at home, but I talked him over and told him we would have no problems at all. At that time the stables were empty, as the landlord had sold all his cows. We could rent the stables from him and the field behind it. I was thrilled! How wonderful! My own horse!

On Television

The phone rang. It was my mother. She did not call me a lot, seldom actually, and we did not visit her a lot. "You are going to be on television tonight! I just saw the advertising spot". "On television, me? What are you talking about?" "Yes, they picked you out of that healing service and a doctor is going to comment." "They cannot do that it is private!" I was so upset.

I went to a special healing service where they prayed for people. Some people were healed, others were not. But I had always believed God for my miracle. Even when other believers told me this would not happen, I stood my ground and told them the opposite. I was actually very annoyed when they spoke to me like that. I believed Jesus was still healing people and today could be the day for mine.

The program was about to start. My husband and I were glued to our seats. I saw myself standing there on the stage trying to ignore a hall filled with people staring at me to see what would happen. I truly believed God could heal me and so I prayed silently for my miracle and fixed my eyes on the man who was going to pray for me. The man looked at me for a few seconds and then said with an angry voice as if he was rebuking me: "You know what you lack? Faith!" The screen switched over to the doctor who commented on what was happening. He said: "Oh so now it is her fault!"

They turned the whole broadcast into a mockery. That doctor was clearly not a believer. The screen was fixed on me again. I was hoping no one could see that my eyes were filled with tears. I left the stage and knew this was purely an attack from the enemy. "I had the most faith of the whole hall!" I shouted at God and at my husband. "They are the ones doubting! How could he say that to me, in front of everyone?" I was so devastated because I did not receive my healing.

While watching "the show" I realized that our neighbours, the people who lived in our street, were probably also watching this. I felt so ashamed, what were they thinking about me now? After all, this program was only broadcast to mock God. I was determined to stand up for my faith and tell them God will still heal me.

The next day I went to the grocery store and the lady said: "I saw you on television yesterday!" Here it was. I don't remember exactly what I said, but I know I wanted to defend God and I spoke words of faith. I looked up biblical scriptures for healing, and I proclaimed them for many years.

Emotional healing

I started to read a lot of Christian books about emotional healing and diligently prayed every prayer from the books and applied in my life what they taught to receive healing. I read my Bible and loved to worship God while turning on the volume of the music. During that time I also sought Christian counselling which I really enjoyed. The lady was very nice and she seemed to truly understand the hurt and rejection I experienced in the past.

2003 – He needs to go

Tears were streaming down my face. I heard my horse calling for me. He was now in a field that he did not know and with other horses he did not know. "Where are you going? Why are you leaving me behind? Wait! Come back!" It was as if I could hear him speak these words through his whinnying. I turned around one last time and he was standing at the gate, ready to come out, his eyes were wide open fixed on me, hoping I would come and get him anyway. I just sold the love of my life.

"Do I really need to sell him? What do you think?" I asked this question to a good friend and to my counsellor. Selling my horse was like ripping out my heart. I had him for six years. We did not have any children, so this horse was my child. He knew me so well. I competed with the horse and made long walks in nature. It took all my energy to take care of him. And it gave me a lot of extra pain; also the stables, field and garden had to be taken care of. My husband was helping me, but I was still doing a lot myself, which I could not do any more physically.

But that was not the main reason why I sold him. My horse was number one in my life. I was number two, then came God and last on the list, my husband. That was not a good order of things. The horse was my idol. I knew if I wanted to have a closer relationship with God and get to know Him better, and if I wanted to love my husband and others as myself, then the horse had to go. My flesh still had to be crucified. My heart was ripped out, but perhaps now God would replace it with a new heart?

"*Then will I sprinkle clean water upon you, and ye shall be clean: from all your filthiness, and from all your idols, will I cleanse you. A new heart also will I give you, and a new spirit will I put within you: and I will take away the stony heart out of your flesh, and I will give you an heart of flesh. And I will put my spirit within you, and cause you to walk in my statutes, and ye shall keep my judgments, and do them.*"
Ezekiel 36:25-27

OUR HOUSE

2005 – A new house & further healing

In September 2005 we moved to another town into our new house that we bought. This was really such a blessing from God, it had a very small garden, but the house was quite spacious and in very good condition. It was all that we needed. We were able to get a social loan, something we could pay off every month. My husband had a good job that he liked.

My back was hurting so severely, that I could hardly sleep anymore. I had to sit up many times during the night because lying down was too painful. For a long period of time, I only got between two to three hours sleep per night. Many times, I had spasms in my legs. These pains were so extreme and sometimes I begged God to just let me die as I could not cope with these pains any longer. We were sleeping on a medical mattress with pressure reducing memory foam and similar pillows.

Also sitting down during the day was very painful, due to a pinched nerve. I had to use an ergonomic seat cushion to be able to sit on a chair. When we were going somewhere, I took it with me. And I couldn't stand up for a long time, as I could not bear the pain in my back. Regularly during the day I had severe cramps around my heart area that made it very painful and hard for me to breath. Luckily these cramps went away after a few minutes. Signs of hernia were showing in my neck. It felt like all the muscles, bones, nerves and tissues in my body were affected.

It was a long process of emotional healing, and it was still difficult for me to be myself and relaxed around people that I knew. I did much better with strangers than with family. Also the pains, mainly the pain in my head caused my social life to be very minimal. Being around people was an effort for me, and after every meeting I was suffering extra pain.

God is my strength
However I didn't want to give any credit to the enemy, and I continued worshiping my Heavenly Father. I had many scriptures I claimed for myself. And my husband kept supporting me. Outside of his working hours, he helped me by doing groceries and cleaning the house.

My father suddenly passed away. It was heart failure. He was only in his fifties. As far as I know, he was not a believer. I still told him the gospel while the machine kept his heart going. But there was no response. It was as if he already died. "I love you papa, I am going to miss you…"

2006 – My mother

"I have to go to the hospital. They are going to take out my eye." "What do you mean, why are they going to take out your eye? Do you mean you going to lose your eye?" "Yes. They found a tumour behind my eye." Sadness filled my heart when I put down the phone. I spoke with the doctor. He told me she had no more than a few months to live. I was shocked. She was diagnosed with an eye melanoma, and the cancer had already spread to her liver.

After the operation we went to my mother's house. She was lying down and it was hard for her to walk around. What happened to her? My husband and I talked about Jesus and the need for being born again, repentance, but she said that she was very sure she would go to Heaven to be with Jesus. I said why are you so sure about that? She answered that she had dreams about her being with Jesus in Heaven.

My husband and I were very worried about her condition, both spiritually and physically, and we invited her to come to our place. My mother agreed, to my great surprise, because she didn't want any treatment. I had forgiven her for everything, because I knew she too was just a victim of deception.

She came with an ambulance and we had prepared a hospital bed for her in the living room. We had no idea how long she would still be with us. But she was very sick. I had to help her to eat and drink, the little bit she could still endure. A nurse came every day to wash her.

"Are you willing to please repeat this prayer after me?" I asked her. She nodded yes. With her last strength she silently prayed a prayer that I had prepared. She passed away the same week that she came to our place. Did she come here with us so she

49

could be saved? I truly hoped that she was now in Heaven.

Thankful

A few weeks after my mother had passed away, I received a clear message from the Lord that I needed to go to her elderly friend, tell him the gospel and he would convert. I had never visited this friend before; nor did I know him very well. I prayed and went to his house. He was an older man, but had been a good friend to my mother for the last years. I shared the gospel with him and he started to cry. In tears he said "I am so thankful that someone finally tells me the truth, because I cannot read the Bible!" He was unlettered. Then he prayed a prayer after me.

I was so thrilled and thankful for this opportunity, because shortly after, he too passed away.

2007 – Horse accident

It had been a long day. My friend was training young horses and riding competitions, so from time to time she was taking private riding lessons and I could join the lesson with one of her horses. This was physically hard for me, sometimes I could hardly walk the following days, because my muscles were hurting so much, but it was worth the pain, as during those hours in the truck, I could talk about God and witness to my friend, and that meant everything to me. I even talked about the end times and things to come. The horses were happy to be back home and longing to go off the truck.

Suddenly one of them kicked open the partition panel in the truck, it hit me very hard and I landed on the ground. It happened so quickly and for a few seconds I did not know what happened. "My knee, it's my knee, but it will be ok." My friend drove me immediately to the doctor. He said this is not ok. You need to go to the hospital. I hated hospitals but had no other choice. My knee was swelling very badly. I called my husband and he came immediately.

The x-ray showed that my anterior cruciate ligament in my knee was completely torn off and not even visible anymore. It had disappeared completely. I also had a meniscal tear. I needed cruciate ligament reconstruction surgery. The recuperation would take about one year.

Healing service

I was one of the last ones to go on the stage. It was around midnight and I was so very tired and in lots of pain. I was full of faith and believed God would heal my knee so that I didn't need to have an operation. A friend from church was willing to go with me and my husband. The long drive in the car had given me lots of extra pain.

Finally it was my turn to go on the stage. His eyes were crossing mine and I was hoping he would not recognize me. This was the same man who told me years ago that I lacked faith. I told him quickly what happened with my knee when he asked me what was wrong with me. Then for a few seconds he laid his hands on me and prayed for me. Before I knew it, someone else was already on the stage. I truly believed this man didn't like me. We went back home and I was sorely disappointed that God did not heal me.

"God, I sought You first for my healing, I went on this long trip because I believed You would heal me. You healed so many people on earth. Why does it never happen to me? I don't want doctors to touch me and have an operation."

The operation

I woke up and asked the nurse why they hadn't started the operation yet? "But you just had the operation" she replied. "It's already done?" I asked in unbelief. "Yes" she said. Shortly after, I started to have tremendous pain in my knee. The morphine they gave me was not working for me, and it made me very sick. I had to throw up the whole night and I felt sorry for the nurse, as I had to call her all the time. In the morning I told her if she wasn't going to take the tube with morphine out of my arm, I would do it myself. She took it out and I felt less sick. The surgeon told me if I was in this amount of pain, I could not go home yet. I told him I would not stay in the hospital any longer and would go home that evening.

The same day, my husband brought me back home and drove the car as slowly as he could. The pain was so intense. The next three weeks were terrible, as I could not take any pain medication. When the manual therapist came, it felt every time as if he was breaking my knee again. I refused to talk to God for three weeks. I was still hurt and upset because I was not healed supernaturally.

Surrender

"Are you ready to talk to Me again?" I heard in my spirit. I said "Yes Lord" and I repented for my behaviour. Who was I to tell God what to do or not to do? He is God and I am not.

" *O taste and see that the LORD is good: blessed is the man that trusteth in him.*" Psalm 34:8

Slowly but steadily my knee began to feel a bit better. After a couple of months I had the courage to ride a horse again. The brace was keeping my knee stable.

Heaven and hell

During my time of recovery I started to be really interested in stories about people who had heaven and hell experiences. I read every story online that I could find and bought books. I read so many stories about Christians being in hell and I wanted to know why? What was their sin? How could Christians end up in hell?

I also began to learn more about the end time, the rapture of the Church, the second coming of Jesus, the mark of the beast, people being left behind, etc. All these things were pretty new to me. But what were most exciting to me were the stories of people who were taken to Paradise and all the beauty that was described and everything that was prepared for the Saints.

"But as it is written, Eye hath not seen, nor ear heard, neither have entered into the heart of man, the things which God hath prepared for them that love him." 1 Corinthians 2:9

"I knew a man in Christ above fourteen years ago, (whether in the body, I cannot tell; or whether out of the body, I cannot tell: God knoweth;) such an one caught up to the third heaven. And I knew such a man, (whether in the body, or out of the body, I cannot tell: God knoweth;) How that he was caught up into paradise, and heard unspeakable words, which it is not lawful for a man to utter."
2 Corinthians 12:2-4

The next years I continued to study the end times, but my true passion was evangelizing. I was always praying and looking for opportunities to be able to share the gospel with someone. I continued to ride horses and shared the gospel with a lot of people that I knew in the horse-world. I gave away books, DVDs, small Gideon Bibles, testimonies about heaven and hell and information about the end times.

Revenge towards the enemy

I was blessed and happy that God gave me so much time to heal from the past. It was still hard for me to be fully relaxed around people. I always got more headaches, many times turning into a migraine, whenever I was talking to someone. The throbbing pain in my head got worse. The more the conversations intensified; the more the band of tension was tightening around my head. It was as if I could not be around people without bearing the consequences of my head acting up. It felt the enemy was still trying to destroy me on all levels, spiritually, emotionally and physically. Why was I such a target for him anyway? I was no one special. I was just a simple housewife who loved God.

However, every time I could witness to someone, was for me a victory, another battle won! I was rejoicing, because in a way it was like taking revenge on the enemy for all he did to me in the past. In fact, the more pain I got in my body, the more passionate I became to find another soul to share the gospel with. I was restricted in what I could do, but determined to do whatever I could and I refused to give in.

I continued to worship my Heavenly Father and Jesus my precious Saviour, because He was the One who made this all possible. I didn't take any pain killers or medicines. Not that this would have been wrong, but medicines simply did not take away any pain in my body, they made me sick. So I had stopped trying long ago. God was my strength and I held on to hope that one day He would heal me.

Counselling

For a period of time I also sought some more counselling. It was the same Christian lady who helped me in the past. I really wanted to be set free from everything and become a better wife.

Our marriage was not bad, but could be much better. I still was not fully emotionally recovered from my past and also the many years of chronic physical pain were not easy.

The liberty to have freedom was manifesting in my life as a spirit of control. I had always been a perfectionist in everything I did, but this type of control was a spirit of slavery. I also needed to learn to set healthy boundaries as I attached myself easily to people and because of this I was too open and vulnerable.

HOPE AND THE GANG

2010 – I Am Coming & the wild Ducks

During 2010, I was in contact with a lot of people online who were also studying the end-times. I felt that God was asking me to spend more time with Him and less with the horse-people. So I did, I reduced my time with the horses to two afternoons per week.

The Lord put me in contact with someone from the United States and in a wonderful way He began to give us messages about preparation for the rapture and tribulation which we shared with others. It turned into a blessed end-time ministry, which reached a lot of people.

"You see those ducks? You could easily hurt them, but they trust their Heavenly Father. Will you also trust Me, no matter what is happening in your life?" I was sitting on a bench in the beautiful woods close by our house and some young wild ducks were sleeping at my feet, which I thought was truly amazing. "What kind of a question is that Lord? Of course I will trust You, no matter what." I was very careful not to make any promises to God, so I said it as a statement. Now I was wondering if something bad was going to happen in my life. Was God preparing and alerting me for something?

Hope and the gang

A group of about 40 wild ducks came running to me, all quacking in their enthusiasm. I parked my bike at the pond and took the box with seeds and grains. This is what they were enthusiastic about. Hope was my favourite duck. Her light brown colour mingled with white, made her unique among the big group. She took the cheese out of my hand, as this was her favourite treat. I called them "Hope and the gang". She was one of the three ducks sleeping at my feet that day when God spoke to me about trusting Him in all circumstances.

"Wow they know you really well!" This comment I received a lot from people walking in the woods. The noisy group of ducks attracted people. Not only did I have a big box of seed but also witnessing packages in my bike. Many people came to me because of the ducks and I took the opportunity to tell them about God's beautiful creations, I witnessed about my faith and told them the gospel. Then I gave them some things to read, including a little Bible. I don't know how many of these precious souls were saved, they were all strangers. I did not know them but I was not there to save them, I was just there to sow my seeds and God would water them and do the rest.

A beautiful testimony

I was full of joy every time I could witness to someone and was praising the Lord on my bike while coming back home. There was an older man that I saw regularly in the woods. He knew me as "the duck-lady". I had prayed to God many times to have an opportunity to witness to him. One day I knew this was the day. He was sitting on a bench and I stopped with my bike to say hi. He was asking me how I was doing and I told him a little bit about my physical condition. He was so surprised to hear this.

"But how is that possible? You always have a smile on your face! I always say to myself when I see you, here is this lady again on her bike and she is smiling again." I thought to myself "Really?" He said "Yes! Your face is always shining." Again I thought "Really?" Now I was surprised to hear this. I gave all glory to God because this was truly wonderful. It was my desire to spread His Light and be His Light. I told him that I prayed for him many times. He had tears in his eyes and said to me "From now on, I will also pray for you". I told him about the love of Jesus for him but that we need to make a choice for Him now and repent of our sins, while we are still alive on this earth.

On another occasion an old man came to me at the pond. I invited him to sit next to me on the bench while I was feeding the ducks. He told me he was in his eighties. Our conversation led to the topic of God and life after death very quickly. He told me that he was not allowed to read the Bible when he was young. "But now you can" I replied. He agreed with me that it was about time to start thinking about life after death. I gave him my witnessing package and he said he would read it all.

These were the things that gave me most joy in my life and kept me going. I live in Belgium, and Christianity here is not large, and thus every opportunity to witness is something to be very thankful for. I kept a list and prayed for these people every day.

2011 – Spring time

I felt the Lord was asking me to give up the horses completely, so I could spend all my time with Him and I did. The end-time ministry with my friend continued to grow very well. And many other people worldwide were giving heed to God's warnings and pleas to stay on the narrow path to be ready for His coming and not be deceived. Little did I know my husband and I were going to fall into a very powerful deception ourselves for the next nine years.

CHAPTER III: END OF FREEDOM

DRAWN AND TRAPPED IN A CULT

THIS FOLLOWING DECEPTION WAS VERY DEEP AND HAS AFFECTED MANY OTHERS. IT HAS BROUGHT A LOT OF HURT AND BROKEN HEARTS IN RELATIONSHIPS. OUT OF RESPECT FOR THE OTHERS, CERTAIN DETAILS WILL NOT BE MENTIONED. ALSO NO NAMES WILL BE USED. PLEASE READ MY TESTIMONY PRAYERFULLY AND TAKE IT TO HEART, AND IF YOU RECOGNIZE SIMILAR THINGS HAPPENING IN YOUR LIFE, YOU MIGHT BE CAUGHT UP IN A DECEPTION OR EVEN A CULT.

The name "Yahushua" is used for Jesus, as this was the name the cult leader taught us to use.

2011 – September 1st - 40-day fast

I just received an email from a lady with a word from God to do a 40-day fast starting September 1st 2011. My husband and I did not see any harm in this and so we agreed to do the fast. This would be our first time that we would do such a long fast. But it was not too hard, we did not eat during the day, but in the evening we had a good meal. Others were also joining in this fast. Much later the lady who sent us the email, told us that we were supposed to do a 40-day water fast. We did not know this.

First contacts

The lady said she had been consecrated with God for two years without any Internet. Only recently did God tell her to go on the Internet and look up "I am coming". This is how she found our ministry and emails, but she was only instructed by God to contact me and not my friend. God told her about me: "She needs lots of healing."

The voice through the phone call spoke the most beautiful words, seasoned with so much passion that it made me feel I was already in Heaven. "Oh Father it is too much, it is too soon, she cannot handle this!" the lady said. Romantic passionate words with a sexual undertone were spoken towards me by Father God through this lady. She called it "Oracling". I felt so privileged that Father God was even interested in me this way. The voice said that there was a special chamber prepared for me in Heaven. Could it truly be that there was sexual intercourse in Heaven with Jesus and Father God? This sure sounded like an invitation to me!

These oracles lasted many hours every week. The lady also spoke personal words over me that were happening in my life or just straight answers to my prayers which she didn't know about, and surprised me every time, and so I truly believed and was confirmed she heard from God and that this was an exceptional lady. She seemed to just understand things without knowing me and she accepted me without judging me.

She even fasted three days with no food or water before she talked to me over the phone call. "Do you have any questions?" she asked me. I always had a paper prepared filled with questions. It amazed me how she could answer them so quickly and easily. Every time the calls ended, I was already looking forward to the next session.

Mysteries from Heaven
She called it "The Mysteries from Heaven". I did not like it when she told me that I could not tell my husband yet. But I obeyed her and kept silent to my husband at this time about the secret things from Heaven. The lady was telling me her life

story and her near death experience and how God saved her life and soul at that time. She shared how she started to fast very soon after her conversion to Christ.

Wow, that was something I had not done. I only fasted a couple of times for a day or half a day in the past. And I did three days water with my friend from the ministry which made me so very sick. I had terrible migraine. The sickness was explained to me by someone else as "deliverance".

Saints and Friends from Heaven

She told me how she had been trained by the Saints in Heaven and how they came down to her in her house. David (The King) was dancing naked in her living room. Kenneth Hagin senior was one of her teachers from Heaven. And there were others. The lady said that God always has one friend on earth and that was Kenneth Hagin when he was still alive. So it was God's friends who were coming down from Heaven in her house to teach and to train her. Now it became clearer to me why she knew so much.

It also seemed such a privilege that these Saints from Heaven came down, and I was reminded of the Saints coming down through my mother in the neighbour's house.

But this is different. This is God and in the past it was the enemy. Look how she is fasting and how fast she grew in God once she was saved and how much she sacrificed. God is so nice to me and those demons from the past were always shouting at me and telling me how bad I was. But God, He has a special chamber prepared for me and all these thoughts ran through my mind.

Mary

"Yahushua talks a lot about you to me. He only speaks good

words." Really? I was so happy to hear this but also very surprised, wow! This was Mary, the mother of Jesus speaking through the lady. She called Jesus "Yahushua".

Fasting

The lady explained that she was always fasting. Especially three day fasts with no food or water before she would minister to someone. I was so impressed but hoping that she would not ask me to do the same. I embraced the idea about fasting, but three days dry fast would be so hard in my physical condition especially with all the headache and migraines.

80 days water fasting

She told me also that God asked her and her husband to do a 40 day water fast. She did it while working full time in a company, but her husband refused and did a Daniel fast instead. Then at the end of 40 days, God asked her if she would be willing to do another 40 day water fast, the fast that her husband refused to do. She said she did it and that made a total of 80 days water fasting. The lady also said she was never hungry when she was fasting, because God had given her a special fasting mantle.

Later she explained that God was looking for people to do such long water fasts, so He could use those fasts for others, but that no one was willing, only she did 80 days of water fasts. I was dumbfounded.

Two witnesses

Because of all the revelations she was receiving and all her fasting, I started to wonder if she and her husband were the two witnesses out of the book of Revelation. I believe God told me that they were and when I asked her, she confirmed it and said "Yes we are the two witnesses."

Wow, now my head was truly spinning! She told me the whole

story how God had made this clear to her. She also explained that many couples had been tested but failed. She and her husband were the only ones who passed their test.

Surrender

Very soon the lady started to talk to me about sexual encounters with God and Jesus. Later she even said that her two little children were not from her husband. The girl was from Yahushua (this is how she called Jesus) and the boy was from the archangel Michael.

She explained how God was not as most people know Him, but that He is in fact a very passionate sexual God and that He and Yahushua desire sexual relationship with their special daughters. And I was one of them. She instructed me to just surrender and let it happen. I felt very uneasy about this. I did it because I didn't want to disobey God and after all she was one of the two witnesses, so I could trust her that she would lead me in the right way.

Ambassadors

"Was that really Yahushua?" I asked her. "Yes she said it was really Him and not an ambassador." "But His face looked like a devil!" I told her one day. "Oh yes Yahushua can come in any form He wants, even like a devil." Now I was ready for a higher level of intimacy with Heaven. Father God would come to me through an ambassador. And the more I grow, the higher the rank of ambassador would come to me and the more intense it would become.

I still hadn't told my husband about these special encounters. But I was hoping to do soon. For now, I just kept it a secret. The lady would tell me when my husband would be ready to know about these things. And I did tell him later about this.

Female side of God.

The lady said that in Heaven everything is different than on earth and what is sin on earth is not sin in Heaven. She meant that a man having sexual relationships with men in Heaven is considered normal. And a woman having sexual relationships with women in Heaven is also considered normal. In fact, she said that everyone in Heaven is naked and everyone is embracing each other. Even the angels are part of this. And even having sex with animals in Heaven is not a sin the lady said.

I remember that my husband wondered about the men's relationship with Jesus, since he is a man. The lady explained that this is a mystery, but she made it seem that there was another part of God in Heaven which is female.

Winter season and Hosea

God continued to give me wonderful opportunities to spread the gospel in the woods and Hope and the gang were my faithful evangelizing partners. Wild geese joined the team and a beautiful big Canadian goose befriended me. I called him Hosea. I worked with him early in the morning while no people were around. Bit by bit I gained his trust and day by day he came closer to me. One day he finally came out of the water. Since then he joined Hope and the gang for the feeding sessions.

Hosea was eating out of my hand just like Hope did. When other people came, he was hiding under the bench where I was sitting until they left. He was so silly and very special and I know God just wanted to give me an extra blessing to keep the smile on my face.

"When was the last time that you saw that goose?" the forester asked me. I was on my way to the pond and it just happened that I hadn't been in the woods for a couple of days. He looked worried and I asked him what was wrong. Then he told me that men were in the woods and had shot many ducks. "They had dogs to get the ducks out of the water. I'm pretty sure they killed and took that big goose also" he said, because I have not seen him since it happened." Hunting in these woods is forbidden. This is a protected nature reservation and people and children are walking everywhere. We assumed they probably did it at night. My heart stood still. Not Hosea. God please not Hosea. Hosea could not fly. He was always near to the pond swimming or just grazing in the field. Oh no! Hope and….

I rushed to the pond. Tears were filling my eyes. The familiar group of ducks were not running towards me this time. The pond looked abandoned, no life at all. "All I have to do is call them" I was thinking. When certain ducks from the group were not around, I had the habit to just call them and they would all come flying to the pond. I called them and for several minutes it stayed very silent. I called again and then I saw some movement on the other side of the pond between the trees. I recognized some of them, but where were Hope and her two men? They moved enough to let me know they heard me, but no one dared to come out of their hiding place. It was clear they had been terrified.

Then I saw this beautiful light coloured duck. It was Hope! She was saved. Pretty soon I saw the whole gang moving around close to each other. Miraculously they were all saved from the shots. I learned that the men had killed mainly the ducks on the other pond. Many were dead on the water. The men had been here also but did not succeed in killing Hope and the gang. It was clear God protected them.

But there was no sign of my beautiful Hosea. I looked everywhere but I knew he was gone. He was probably sold and eaten for Christmas dinner. This time I was not singing on my bike on my way back home.

Hosea in Heaven

It was time for another session on the phone with the lady. I just found out about Hosea and couldn't stop my tears. I told her what happened and the lady immediately had a vision about Hosea in Heaven and that I would have him back in Heaven. Oh this gave me great consolation!

January 2012 – Another fast

It was time for another fast. This time I did a 40 day juice fast. The lady also thought it was a good idea for us to do strong warfare prayers. Every day my husband and I sat on the floor, put our tallit around our head and prayed the long list of warfare prayers. She also told us that she and her husband were sitting on the floor holding each other's hand and rocking back and forth while praying. She said we should do the same thing. This was very weird for us and we tried it a couple of times, but did not succeed to do this continually.

The Last Call Letters

The ministry with "I Am Coming" was still going very well and more than a thousand people had subscribed to the email list to receive the messages from God. Daily, my friend and I received many emails from people who were blessed by the letters. We had built up some beautiful relationships and were planning to meet with some of our online friends soon.

The lady was asking me to send "The Last Call Letters" that she was receiving from God with the "I am coming" letters to our email list. My friend and I started doing this around March. These new letters were totally different in tone and style. I started to feel insecure about the messages I received from God, when I compared them with these letters from "The Last Call".

March 2012 – A new website
"You have three weeks to build a website. It needs to be finished beginning of April." This was my first assignment I received from the lady and it was a serious one. First of all building a website in three weeks from scratch seemed impossible to me, and besides that, I knew nothing about building websites! A tremendous amount of pressure came on me. But I wanted to obey God and prayed for His help and leading.

I looked up information online about building a website, found a Christian host, gathered information about getting ready for Jesus, how to be saved, prayers etc. and of course a section for God's Last Call Letters. I managed to get it ready before the deadline and thus "YHWH GLORY END TIME MINISTRY" was born.

The last "I am Coming"
Meanwhile a worldwide 40 day fast was proclaimed in the newest Last Call Letter that the lady received. My friend and I from the ministry were willing to do the fast, but my friend did not agree to send it out in the "I am coming" letters. The lady told me to send her letter out via an email service provider to the subscribers of "I am coming". For me it felt like stealing the subscribers, as these people all subscribed to "I am coming" and not to "The Last Call".

The lady told me God knew this would happen and that was the reason why I had to build this new website so quickly. I thought this was amazing, but then I was very sad to hear when the lady told me that I had to break all ties with my friend in the U.S. The lady had never contacted my friend.

This was the end of "I am coming". A beautiful ministry and friendship was abruptly broken. In one moment I lost all my online friends. In a way I could not believe it, as it all went so fast. There was no time to think a lot about it, as the lady was preparing to leave the U.S. and come visit us in Belgium.

I will miss them

Many times, my friend and I would talk for hours over the phone. We shared very personal things and we prayed together. It just clicked between us from the very beginning. The lady told me that people were dying because they were judged by God. Later she said that my friend would suffer greatly during the tribulation and die as a martyr. Because she did not agree with the Last Call message that proclaimed a worldwide 40 day fast. The lady called my friend a witch.

April 2012 – She is coming!

"You look like a witch" I said to the lady when I picked her up from the airport in Brussels. "But I am supposed to look like a witch" she replied. She was tall and super skinny. It was obvious she had been fasting a lot. They brought lots of big suitcases and duffle bags. Here she was the lady and her husband, the two witnesses, and together with their two little children they were going to stay with us. What an honour I thought. The lady had two other teenage sons, which stayed with her first husband in the U.S. I thought that the two witnesses would be perfect, but this lady had to be born again, fast, repent, was divorced, re-married and had four children.

But who was I to judge what was right or wrong? She brought many fancy clothes and lots of shoes. These were from the time when she was still working as a business manager.

Control

We gave them our biggest bedroom and had extra mattresses on the floor for the children. The man didn't say a lot. He was mostly quiet and prayed in the Spirit all the time. I learned that he was on assignment with the archangel Michael and they were doing warfare together in the heavenlies. This was all done in the spirit. He was smoking and was hiding his cigarettes in the house.

From the first moment they arrived, the lady took control over our house and over us. The man didn't like me. He told the lady he didn't want to come to this house, because I was a witch. "You are beating him up! Michael is telling me!" I stood speechless on the ground when I heard this. The lady was referring to the spirit of control that was reigning in me towards my husband. But I know she was right. I was not a good wife for my husband. He didn't take control, so I did it. Everything had to be exactly the way I wanted it to be.

I was careful and felt guilty whenever I went to the woods, as I had the impression the lady was not approving of it. She lived in a totally different world. In a way I was a disappointment to them. I imagined the two witnesses to be very different.

Nevertheless I cooked fresh food for them every day. I remember the man was always happy to eat and waiting at the table whenever the food was cooking on the stove.

Strange stories

"I think Father will be ok that I break my Esther fast sooner" she replied when I asked her if she had forgotten about our special dinner that evening. I had ordered a big cheese platter for our guests with special breads and fruit. At the table, my husband and I heard things that we never heard before.

The man was telling us that he never wanted to go to Paradise, because it is too boring there. The lady replied, "Well, it is beautiful. It is Jesus' planet and a reward for His obedience at the Cross." This sounded disrespectful to me. Jesus got a reward that was not even that special? I remembered all the stories that I read how people had visions about Paradise and how wonderful and amazing it was over there. Now I heard it was nothing special. "If Father decides in the end to throw me in hell, then He will do that!" the lady said. I was thinking how could this happen, since she was so obedient and full of surrender all the time? Then what would He decide about me in the end? "And after everything is finished on this earth, it will all begin again" the man said.

"God will just use a new planet and we will come back and start all over again." Now I was really discouraged. "It is just a game for Father between good and bad" the lady said. "So there is no eternal rest and hope for that?" I asked. "You just start all over again on a new planet" was the response. The lady and man said that their youngest children would be man and wife on the next planet.

I was dying inside but our guests seemed to just have accepted all this. This sounded to me like reincarnation as my mother taught me.

Ambassadors

They also told me that Father had a wine cellar in heaven and sometimes He got drunk when things got too much for Him and when He just wanted to distance Himself from these things. The angels were writing down everything that happened on earth, and God looked in the books to see what was happening. "Why do you think God has ambassadors?" she asked me. "Because they take His place on the throne to do His work. All the people who say they have seen God in heaven; it is really an ambassador they saw. There are many different levels of ambassadors in heaven, but the ones who take God's place, look exactly like Him. Why do you think Yahushua is omnipresent? Because He has many ambassadors on earth and in heaven."

Again I felt this was so disrespectful towards the Lord, as they described Him as someone who is really not that special. Yet He was their best friend. It shook me up, as everything I ever learned about God and Jesus being almighty and omnipresent, was robbed in one moment.

I concluded that I did not know God at all and that He was very different than I thought He was.

Yahushua sinning

But the most astounding thing she told us was that even Yahushua had to make sacrifices in heaven for His sins. "What! Yahushua sins?" I replied. "Oh yes He does!"

The hairdresser

"Watch and learn" she said to me. The hairdresser was cutting the lady's long and thick hair. I could see he was very fascinated by her, when he was listening to her story and how she was a missionary from the US.

Then when she said her goodbyes, she hugged him. She explained to me, this is the way to do it, by touching people we could touch them with God's glory. Ok, this was a new revelation to me.

Another lady

Around May another lady from the U.S came to our house with more suitcases and duffle bags. She took care of the children. She was the handmaiden. She had left her husband and three young daughters behind to follow the lady. I did not understand how the maiden could be so ok with that, and why she did not even cry for her children and husband? She said she had a good marriage and that her husband was even her best friend. But she just left, as she believed the lady was part of the two witnesses and it was her calling to follow the lady. She wanted to be very close to the lady and was even sitting on the floor at the bedroom door, when the lady was resting.

One day she was rebuked by the lady in my presence. The lady told the handmaiden that she had to follow my example and ask God every little detail, like I was doing. "Good job very well done!" I got my first compliment and was so happy to hear God was pleased with me.

Pretty soon our house became very messy and the kitchen was always dirty. They just left all the dishes overnight in the sink and in the morning there was a pile for me to clean up. I also noticed the bedroom they used smelled really bad. They never opened the window to refresh the room. It was the same smell that all of their clothes had.

House clean-up

"Father wants to have an altar in the centre of the living room, so when you come in, this is the first thing that you see." The lady started to change our living room and moving all the furniture around. "Father hates that mirror!" she shouted at me. It was a mirror that we bought many years ago at a country fair. My husband and I liked it very much and it was just beautiful against the natural wall. She also instructed us that we could never change the living room. It had to stay this way as this was how Abba wanted it.

We had a car loaded with things ready for the recycling including the mirror. I was hoping we could keep the cabinets and our leather seats in the living room. We had to search carefully at the time to find these comfortable ones, and they were perfect to support my back and neck. Fortunately they could stay as leather does not hold deliverance the lady said. The lady went through our house and showed us everything that had to go. We had a big collection of worship CDs. All these had to go, as the singers were not right with God the lady said.

This was not the first time we had to throw things away in and around our house. In 2011, my friend from "I Am Coming" and I were contacted by a man from Africa. This man said he was assigned by God to monitor my friend and me. He had a wild story that he was a snake in the past, but got delivered from that. Then he told us that we could never withhold ourselves from our husbands to have sex. I asked him what he did when his wife was not in the mood or didn't feel good? "I rape her" he said. This man told us we could not have any statues or images from animals. My husband and I broke off the little birds from the bird feeders outside and anything else we encountered. The man also commanded my friend and I to fast.

In August 2011 the man told us that we all had to meet online every night at 12 to do warfare, even other believers worldwide were joining us. This was very hard for me and my husband, as the meeting lasted for many hours, till 4 or 5am. My husband had to go to work and I was full with migraine. We did this every night during the month of August. Some of us saw visions from heaven and also demons everywhere. Was this all correct or was this deception?

When the lady began to talk with me in September 2011, she said this man from Africa was deceiving the bride deliberately and trying to exhaust her. My husband and I were relieved that we didn't have to get up anymore in the middle of the night to do warfare. But he was disappointed as he realized the visions he received from heaven were probably false.

Neighbours complaining

The doorbell rang. It was one of our neighbours telling us that his wife couldn't sleep as she heard bouncing noise all night, like someone running up and down the stairs. They could also hear a lot of noise on the street coming from the main bedroom. I felt so ashamed and bad. All those years we tried to keep a good relationship with our neighbours. We even witnessed to them one day about us being Christians and our faith in Jesus. What kind of a witness were we now?

The noise on the stairs was from the little boy who was running up and down all night. He never slept during the night. And the noise that could be heard on the street was coming from all of them, as they were all staying in the room upstairs at the street. One day the elderly neighbour woman was taken to the hospital. The lady said she was judged by God with a heart problem, because she was talking bad about her.

This brought more fear to me and I was thinking "I better make sure I have no wrong thoughts about the lady anymore."

People marked

The lady had a special gift. She could see a mark on people's forehead if they were saved. It scared me as most of the people of our town were not showing any mark. Her gift to see this, made me very uncomfortable and every time she looked at me, I wondered if she still saw the mark on my forehead.

Missing

One day the lady's husband was missing. We searched the whole house. Then we found out someone called the police as he was sitting at the edge of the main street, praying in the spirit and rocking back and forth. They probably thought he was someone who had escaped from the mental institution a bit further up the road. He and the lady were fighting a lot. He called her some bad and ugly names. This made me wonder even more about the two witnesses. They were just humans in the flesh, like my husband and I.

Escaping

My time in the woods became my escape trips from home. I did not like what was going on in our house. These people were different and it felt that I did not fit in their world. I was hoping they would leave soon. I was counting the hours until my husband would be back from work, as he had a fulltime job. The lady and the handmaiden were very close to each other. Many years later the handmaiden told me that she and the lady did a blood covenant in our house. The two ladies were up all night and slept in the morning hours. I was trying to be as quiet as I could when I woke up. During those times I cleaned up the house. The lady always woke up the handmaiden who was sleeping on the couch in the living room.

Esther fast

The handmaiden was also super skinny because of anorexia. She and the lady were not eating a lot and every time I did, I felt guilty and tried to eat without them seeing it. I kept some cookies in my office. Every week, we all had to do three days dry fasting. They called it Esther fasting. My husband and I were counting the hours until midnight so we could finally break the fast. We had our snacks ready upstairs next to our bed. The ladies didn't seem to bother a lot about food.

The lady came upstairs and sat next to me on our bed. Suddenly she was throwing up all over our bed. "Oh I am so sorry. This is the deliverance from all of you." "It is ok, I will clean it up…" was my response to her. Many times she got sick because she was delivering the demons in us. I felt guilty as she had to go through so much because we were so defiled, and especially me, since the old woman in me had been called out as a witch.

Scrolls from heaven

In the morning, I always made a nice breakfast for the lady and brought it to her, while she was sitting on the terrace. I made sure it was all ready when she came out of the bathroom. It was such an honour to be able to make food for God's witnesses. I always wondered why my husband and I were chosen to be the ones to host them.

Every morning, the lady read the scroll from heaven that the angels showed her. Wow, I thought, that is so amazing. On the scrolls were all the assignments for that day. Even if she was supposed to just have a talk with me, then that was also written on the scroll.

She was talking about the end times and how Michael would easily make a big hole in the floor of our house, where we could shelter in times of need. Then I felt honoured that Michael was so present with us too. She told us to buy canned food and keep a stock of extra water.

We learned so much about keeping the Biblical feasts, anointing ourselves every day for protection, the daily warfare prayers, cleansing our house with the blood of Yahushua, and mainly fasting to receive our deliverance from the old persons. We also had to learn to be led by the Spirit and not by our flesh.

Visiting my aunt

The lady decided to visit my aunt. My aunt had moved around 1996, as she wanted to live closer to us. I remember my aunt did not like the lady. "She has a big spirit of death above her" the lady said. "She will not live much longer." My husband and I visited my aunt regularly during all those years. But every time we tried to talk to her about God, she changed the subject. She just refused to submit to God and wanted to live her life as she desired it although she was baptized and came to the Church that we attended for a short period of time. After that she never went to Church anymore. I remember I wrote her a letter that clearly said if she would not surrender and give her heart to Jesus that she would go to hell.

Quitting work

"Oh I am so happy we don't have to leave our house and country." These were my thoughts when I heard the lady talking about many in the U.S. who moved to Ecuador to look for a safe haven. "Oh" she said, "I have a vision, you two need to go also!" In one moment I was totally hopeless. This couldn't be. Us moving to Ecuador? "Yes" she said, "and you will never come back ever again."

We were sitting in the house of my husband's employers. The woman cried when we told her the news. Everyone liked my husband and he was a good worker. He had worked in their company for ten years. It was hard to quit his job, as my husband really liked it. He had good colleagues and a good salary.

So sorry

With a heavy heart I stepped into my aunt's apartment. I had no courage to tell her we were leaving the next month to Ecuador, forever. She didn't understand and was very hurt and angry. She was in her eighties and we just left her alone. She had no one else to take care of her. I felt so selfish but I had to obey God and trust Him that He would take care of her.

My first serious rebuke

"Please don't shout so hard, I can hardly focus on driving anymore." The lady shouted even harder at me, she was screaming while we were in the car on our way to Brussels to renew the passports for traveling. I had some things on my heart about the handmaiden and I just wanted to talk to the lady about this. I was shocked at her response. She said God was so angry at me and it was Him rebuking me while screaming at me.

ECUADOR

End of June 2012 –No goodbye's

With tears in my eyes I said my goodbye to my friends in the horse stable. Although it was a year since I last rode a horse, I still visited my friends to talk or to witness to them.

We were not allowed to say goodbye to our family. We just wrote a short letter that we were leaving the country but we could not say where we were going. They had no idea what was going on until they received the letter. By then we were already gone.

My husband, I, the handmaiden and the children stepped into the taxi. Our neighbour, a car mechanic, was looking at us. He had become a good friend to me. I had witnessed a lot to him and many times I was there in the weekends to take care of his horses when he was not around. For some time, I was giving riding lessons to his girlfriend.

One last look at the mechanic and with a heavy heart I stepped into the taxi. This was going to be the last time I saw our house and our neighbours. They had no idea we were leaving. It was still early in the morning. Everything inside of me screamed "Don't do it, don't go!" But I could not give in to my flesh and keep holding on to things. After all, God was very angry at me and I was rebuked hard by him in the car that day. So I had to pass this major test that God was putting us through.

Leaving

I was overloaded with more suitcases than allowed as I wanted to take as much as I could. The lady and her husband were staying in our house in Belgium. Their test was to let their children go with us to South America and God told the lady that she would never see her children again. The handmaiden would take care of them. The lady and her husband had the keys of our house and our car. She told me I had to ask the mechanic to buy our car and even my saddle that I always used to ride the horses. We had an agreement he would take over our car when the lady and her husband would leave our house. Then he would receive the key from the house and come to water the plants and look for any important mail. We didn't know what was going to happen to our house.

A friend of my husband was going to come from time to time to take care of our little garden. Later he told us that he always saw the man smoking in the garden and the children playing. The children playing? The children were not even in Belgium anymore, they were with us in South America. How could you have seen the children playing in our garden? "No no, the children were there with the lady and the man, I saw them in the garden." This was such a strange thing. Was he not supposed to know that the children left with us? Was this a vision the angels gave him to let him believe the children were still in our house with their parents? Later (once we had returned) the mechanic told me he never saw the children getting into the taxi, only us and the handmaiden. He thought the children just stayed in our house with their parents. Wow, for sure something weird had happened with those children.

Troubles

The trip was not blessed, as we had delays at the airport, and we had to pay a lot of money for the extra luggage. Finally, we got through the border control and we were off to Cuenca, a long flight.

My husband and I could rent an apartment and the handmaiden and the children were renting a different apartment. It was the end of June and we were fasting.

July –Visions and a strange manifestation

During the month of July my husband and I were praying about serious things from the past and he suddenly received a wound in his foot for about a week. After a week, when we finished praying, the wound closed quickly and disappeared. What a weird supernatural manifestation! The revelations were that I had been abused by seven men (family and people I knew) when I was about four years old. We believed this was true and it was also explaining why I felt emotionally the way I did. We asked the lady and she confirmed all this indeed truly happened. I never had received revelations like this before. I had no memories at all about all this and then doubt came in my heart. Did this really all happen to me?

Attacked

The door from the oven flew open and the power that came out was so strong that it threw me violently backwards against the wall. My whole body was paralyzed and I thought I was dying. Later the lady told me this was an attack from the enemy and Michael the archangel stepped in and received most of the blow to save me. Oh wow, I was so thankful for that. Good to know Michael was on my side.

Clothes

The handmaiden came over. We were always looking forward to her coming to find out if there was any news from the lady. She was the only one who was in contact with her. But we were also stressed because we could get rebuked. The handmaiden told me I had to get rid of all the extra clothes that I brought. This was a nice rebuke. I could keep one or two outfits. I threw away the nice warm clothes that I really liked. I bought them in a horse shop and they were very good quality. God was really stripping me of everything.

Separated

I loved my husband very much, but he had been in a depressive mood for a long time. He told me many times he just wanted to go to Heaven. I couldn't handle it very well, though I tried to encourage him. I was making a lot of effort to always be in a positive mood, despite the pain I had in my head and body, but I still refused to give in and did not want to show any weakness or dejection towards the devil. Witnessing to people, talking about my faith, worshiping God, animals and nature were helping me to "just keep going" in the constant physical pain I was in. Just even the headache all the time was unbearable.

Deep down in me I was always afraid to lose my husband. My past with my mother had taught me that I had to break all relationships with the people that I loved or were closest to me. So I figured if I kept my distance a bit from my husband, then I would not have to break with him. At least he was with me now in South America.

My husband and I could not be together in one room. We each had our own room and we were hardly together during the day. We stayed in our rooms with closed doors and repented for being so attached to our country, our house, to friends, people we knew, all the familiar places. I was definitely not ready to be a missionary! We repented for every detail we could think of. I never learned how to truly repent until now. When I was born again, I only felt happiness, I did repent, but I was never so broken and in tears on my face for all the sin in my life. Now, in this brokenness, I truly repented from my heart. And even much deeper repentance would come later.

I only got out of the apartment to use the internet café a bit further up the street, to see if there were any new instructions from the lady, and sometimes I had to send out a Last Call Letter to the email list.

Sad and broken

The hours passed so slowly and we were so weak. How long did we had to stay here, locked up in an apartment, only repenting and crying out to God. I missed my husband so much, though he was only one door away from me. One night I had a strange meeting. I saw in the spirit a man on top of me and he looked like God or Jesus. He made love with me. I told the lady and she told me I had been misled and was now infected with the Kundalini spirit, which is very hard to cast out.

I didn't understand as the lady encouraged me while I was still in Belgium to do these things and she always confirmed it was indeed Jesus and Father God, when I shared these encounters with her. I always asked her, as I didn't want to be misled.

Even the handmaiden had just shared with me about her sexual encounters with angels and Father God. Then she heard that she had the Kundalini spirit also, as she made love with a young man who was staying with them in their apartment even though this was done under instruction from the lady. Her test was to disobey the instruction and not make love with him. But she failed.

September – More fasting

We fasted so hard during this time, we did seven days Esther fast (no food or water), seven days Communion fast, and seven days Esther fast again. This all was to purify and cleanse us and make us ready for Yahushua's coming. Every night we did warfare. The lady told us that a special place was prepared in this environment of Ecuador by Michael the archangel to house the 144,000. I guess we were just waiting until we were ready to go to that place.

I looked out from the little window in my room. My only view was the old houses. I was longing for the woods and wondered how Hope and the gang were doing. A friend that I met in the woods agreed that she would feed them the seeds and grains I gave her. I was hoping she would keep her promise.

I also thought about my aunt. How was she doing all by herself? I was not allowed to contact her or anyone else in Belgium. She was still strong when we left. She loved me but had a hard time showing her emotions towards me, so she did it by giving us things whenever we needed something, and blessing us financially. I recognized myself in her, because I also had a hard time showing my emotions to the people that I loved. My mother and father had the same problem. I cannot remember that they ever gave me a hug or a kiss. But thanks to my aunt we were also able to buy our house and thus get a loan that was affordable. God had been good to us.

I had to repent for having these thoughts and longings now, as the whole purpose was also to detach us completely from our loved ones, friends and things that we liked. There could be no more desires. "Oh God please help us!"

There was a river nearby and on Rosh Hashanah I went over there to throw some breadcrumbs in the water. This represented throwing away my sins.

The park

I also noticed there was a park nearby. I convinced my husband to come with me for a walk over there. Finally some grass and green! It was a nice place, but I started to think about the woods in Belgium. Here guards were always walking around and my husband did not like to come to this park because of the guards. We noticed they were watching us as they could see we were strangers. We found some ducks and I gave them a piece of a cracker which they fearlessly took out of my hand. They were used to being fed by visitors.

I did not like it at all here in this town. In fact, I hated it. Everything was old and dirty. And I was not happy to be stuck inside an apartment with nothing to do, except for repenting, fasting, doing warfare and crying out to God for deliverance. There was no happiness at all. We never had a smile on our faces. Whatever was left from that smile back in Belgium had now died completely. Being here felt like hell to me.

On our way back we passed a bakery, just an open shop with a few pastries. "You want to have one?" I asked my husband. He said "No, we are not allowed, we will be rebuked."

No more income

I noticed that the money I received monthly from the health insurance did not appear anymore in our account. I called them and heard that I ignored the invitation to go for my yearly medical examination. I did not even know about this. The person who took care of our mail had not informed me about that letter.

Fortunately, another couple from the U.S. joined us in Cuenca and they paid for our rent over there for that month. We never knew how we would pay. But somehow it always worked out. "You can have these for free!" the lady on the market told us when she happily put some extra fruit in the bag. It was a steep road up to the market place. We only had a few dollars to buy some food. God blessed us through this nice Ecuadorian lady.

All alone

We had to find a cheaper apartment. Eventually we could move into an apartment upstairs in the same building. The owners were very nice. They lived next door and sometimes I visited them if I needed to use their computer to check for emails or do some work on the website. I loved to watch their garden as it had some nice plants and a lovely parrot. The woman helped us with practical things and she even took us in her car from time to time to go to the shops if we needed things. I took advantage of the opportunity and told her about Jesus. I always tried to convince her and her husband that we were all happy and were sent to this country as missionaries.

"Please don't leave me here all alone." My husband and

someone else who stayed with us were instructed by the lady to move into the house of the handmaiden. My husband looked at me but he had to obey God and go. I probably never showed more despair in my eyes as then. I watched through the window how he put his suitcase in the taxi and then he was gone.

I was all alone in the apartment. I was not allowed to go to the house where everyone else stayed. I was not ready they told me. I still needed too much deliverance. Was I really so much worse than the others? Since the handmaiden arrived in our home in Belgium, I always felt excluded from them.

I did my very best to continue in prayers and warfare during the day and night, but I missed my husband so much, and I was afraid I would never see him again. I did not feel safe all alone in this apartment and on the street, in a strange country where I did not even understand the language, as most spoke Spanish.

From whence cometh my help...
"I will lift up mine eyes unto the hills, from whence cometh my help. My help cometh from the LORD, which made heaven and earth." These words from Psalm 121, I said so many times when I looked out of the window in the bedroom that had a view out to the mountains. I cried and cried out to God in desperation day and night, because I thought I would be left behind forever here and never see my husband or anyone else ever again. I didn't even know where they were.

You will go back
I had my face on the floor crying out to God and repenting. I heard in my spirit that I would return to Belgium. This sounded like music to my ears, but I rebuked the thought. However, the thought was so strong in me that I went to the internet café to

check for any messages. There was a message from the handmaiden that it was time to return to Belgium and that my husband could also go with me. I could not believe what I was reading, so I read it again and again, to make sure I was not mistaken. I was so very happy!

I also got a message that my aunt has passed away. Oh no. I got in contact with my half-brother and he arranged money for us to book a flight.

My husband came back to the apartment. He was not as excited as I was because he thought we had failed our test. We connected online with the handmaiden and the lady. She was in Israel with her husband and all happy and told us that we passed our test and we could now return to Belgium. This was the best news ever! She also said that God deliberately separated me from my aunt, as she was not right with God.

New names

The lady had given us new names as the old names were evil she said. She called my real birth name "the old woman" and my husband's birth name was "the old man". The goal was to get rid of our "old persons" by fasting and receiving our deliverance, so that these new spirits that were assigned to us could take over our body. It was even a test for these spirits from heaven to be able to earn a body. And it was our test to be found worthy to be inhabited fully by these spirits. If we would fail, the spirits would be taken away from us. The lady told us that these spirits from heaven were perfect and pure, so whenever we were manifesting the old persons, we had to repent and continue to fast in order to be delivered. "Layer by layer, like peeling an onion" she explained to us.

But it would take many years for us, since the lady herself had to go through this process also back in the U.S. And even now, from time to time, she still had to be healed from certain things. She taught us that most Christians did not even receive this type of deliverance, as most did not want to fast so intensely as we did, and most were not doing warfare as we did.

Counting

We were instructed to leave the apartment without saying anything to our landlords next door. We could only leave them a note. I felt so very uncomfortable about this, because it just did not feel right. But we had to obey and did as we were told. We took our things downstairs as silently as we could. It was still early in the morning, so they were probably still sleeping. I was so stressed and hoping they would not notice anything.

Finally, we got our stuff in the taxi and we were on our way to the airport. I was so happy to be out of this town and country. My husband warned me not to fall into the same sin and "old woman" behaviour as before. No more attachments and no more control.

But I smelled freedom and I was overjoyed. Our dinner in the plane looked delicious. It was a stew with chicken in cream sauce. My husband did not touch the chicken as we were not allowed to eat meat. But I could not resist it and ate it. Was I already sinning? I would probably be rebuked for this? Why could I just not obey God in this and why did my husband have more discipline than me? I was disappointed in myself.

BACK TO BELGIUM

November 2012

After 4 ½ months in Cuenca we came back to the familiar street in Belgium. There was a stack of mail lying on the ground in the hallway. It looked like this had not been taken care of for a long time. Oh it was so good to be back! I just couldn't believe it. And we passed our test. That was the greatest thing! Although my husband continued to believe that we had failed our test in Cuenca and therefore we were sent back to Belgium. I felt sad as he could not rejoice in us being back.

The house looked nice. "At least they cleaned it up" I thought. The lady and her husband left our house in August when they went to Israel. Our friend had done a good job in the garden too. Everything was nicely trimmed. "She is really weird" one of the neighbours said. He was talking about the lady, ironically enough I agreed with him, but didn't dare to say anything negative.

I was trying to give all the clothes and shoes they left a place. I hung them nicely in a wardrobe. The same bad smell was filling the wardrobe. These clothes were really stinky.

The Counsellor

I found the letter from the medical counsellor. My appointment had already expired many weeks ago. Immediately I made a new appointment as we still had no income. The handmaiden instructed me "Tell the counsellor this and that." I was annoyed and was thinking "You don't need to tell me what to say, I am capable enough to do this myself." I explained to the counsellor that I was so very sorry that I missed the appointment, and told him about our missionary trip to Cuenca. I just told him the truth. It was a miracle from God that he approved me again and my income was restored.

My half-brother and the Christian church had arranged the funeral for my aunt. Everything was done when we came back. I was sad because I could not be there for her. I could only hope she had taken a right decision in the end.

But the lady said she was in hell. I was thinking "If I would have been there for her, maybe this would not have happened?" The lady also said that I had to throw away everything my aunt ever gave us. But we could keep my aunt's money, the inheritance. So my husband and I went through our house again and threw away everything my aunt gave us. The inheritance money went to the lady in Israel. Among other things, she bought 30 pieces of silver with this money. When I heard that, it felt to me like a betrayal of our Saviour Jesus, like Jude did. She said we could never tell this to anyone, but that God was so pleased that we did it. But "we" had no idea she was going to do this. And she was going to present these coins to Yahushua when He comes.

No contact
Though we were back, we were not allowed to contact any of the family or friends. No one could even come to our house, everyone had so many demons and it would disturb the holiness. The lady had anointed our house when she was still here and now everything was purified.

"You can stay in the hallway but not come in the living room." My half-brother did not understand this, but accepted it without any further discussion. He just wanted to talk about some things.

Back in the woods
"Come! Come!" I was shouting. Hopefully the ducks had not forgotten me. There they were! I saw Hope on the water with some others. I had food with me, but Hope refused to come out of the water. She totally ignored me. "Was it because the old woman was here?" The other ducks were following Hope. I felt

so bad.

The next few days I kept trying. Eventually, after several days, Hope came out of the water and was willing to eat the food out of my hand. The others from the group came also and I could see everyone was still there.

"They refused to eat anything once you left" my friend in the woods said to me. "I called them and they never came out of the water." Wow!

"Hope has never has eaten anything. She was grieving for you" the lady said. Another Wow, Hope did not even come to the lady? She told me, once we left to Cuenca, that she and her husband took our bikes and went to the woods every day to see Hope. But Hope never came to them. So good to see Hope and the gang restored again!

January 2013

It was freezing cold. I had a blanket around me and was sitting upstairs on the second floor. I was banned here for several weeks after a rebuke. I could only have communion and water. In the evening for lunch I received half of a fried onion. My husband and the other young lady, who had been with us in Cuenca, were eating more. I did not dare to go to the woods during this time, as I did not want to challenge God. Everything was so serious and I needed my deliverance from "the old woman".

April 13, 2013

The non-profit organization YHWH-GLORY-END-TIME-MINISTRY was established here in Belgium. This was an assignment for us from the lady. Three people were part of it, me, my husband and his good friend who took care of our garden.

The ministry received a lot of donations, we tried to use a bank account linked to the organization, but it always failed. We had to change banks four times, as every bank closed our account because of the huge amounts that came in from abroad. The lady and her handmaiden had our bank card and were taking out a lot of money abroad. They were still in Israel. All this looked very suspicious to the banks here in Belgium, and I had to call them all the time to explain things or sort things out. But the lady always said not to worry and that God would protect us all, which He did.

Lots of work

There was a lot of administration work to do for me to keep all these finances up to date in my records. I had to pray hard and learn how to do this as at the end of the year it all had to go to an accountant to check everything. It required a lot of creativity to put every single transaction on our accounts in the correct section. I had to add lots of explanations to explain away the unusual way of working.

The lady did not care. I had to figure it all out myself. But gladly all was accepted well with the accountant at the end of the year. I also had to keep the website up to date and send out "The Last Call Letters" regularly to the email list.

I didn't like anything I was doing, and was discouraged to hear this was my calling and only the beginning of my testing. Nevertheless, I wanted to please God and did everything with much zeal and excellence. My husband and I had to stay separated as much as possible in the house so we could both receive our deliverance. We were told not to have sexual contact, as this would disturb our deliverance process. I was basically living in the office and my husband stayed in our bedroom upstairs during the day, as he had a desk there. Sometimes he sent me a little message in my email to encourage me.

Fasting

We continued to fast all the time. Every week three days Esther fast (dry fast) and the long fasts in January, April, July and September. But there was always a reason to fast. I counted the days one time and we were fasting more days per year than we were eating.

"Remember Ananias and Sapphira"

Acts 5:3,5: But Peter said, Ananias, why hath Satan filled thine heart to lie to the Holy Ghost, and to keep back part of the price of the land? And Ananias hearing these words fell down, and gave up the ghost: and great fear came on all them that heard these things.

These words were spoken to me a lot to make sure we gave all the money from our income and from the ministry. We could keep what we needed to pay our costs, but everything else and all extra income had to go to the lady. I didn't understand why this Scripture was repeated so much to me, as I was very honest with the money and would not have kept even one cent. It hurt me that the lady repeated this so much to me. If she did not trust me, then why was I responsible for all the money affairs?

I did not like doing the finances anyway. But she said it was my job to do it and I had better make sure I remembered Ananias and Sapphira.

Our neighbour

"Come out of the bathroom, quickly!" I said to the young lady who lived with us. "But I am in the bath." "It doesn't matter you need to sing to our neighbour, he is here!" I replied. Our neighbour was a sweet man who was living by himself. His only companion was his parrot. I had witnessed to him many times. In the beginning he used to run away from me, "No! She is going to preach to me again" he said and off he ran. From time to time he rang our doorbell and then we had a discussion because I didn't want to take back the reading material I gave him about Jesus. He was really nice, but he did have an alcohol problem and he did not take good care of himself.

"You think I will go to Heaven? Are you still praying for me?" he asked me one day. "Yes I still pray for you, every day and you are even the first one on my list." "I don't believe that" he replied. "Come and see" I said. I showed him my prayer list and his name was first on my list. He was so touched and amazed. He told me I was the only one who always sent him a card on his birthday.

Here he was in our living room. My friend came out of the bathroom, and she started to sing a blessed song to him. Her voice was very beautiful. It was in English but it sounded very nice. "She is mentioning my name" he said to me, with a big smile on his face. I said "Yes, it is a special song for you." The man was really blessed and I am sure no one had ever sung to him like this before. These were the rare blessed times.

THEY'RE BACK

August 2013

I picked up the lady, her handmaiden and the children from the airport in Brussels. They all came back from Israel. I was not enthusiastic or happy that they were coming back, but I did not show this. In fact we learned to just pretend we were happy in her presence. "Look!" she said, "one month pregnant and I already look like three months!" The lady showed me her belly in the toilets. I was like "Wow, it does indeed look like you have been pregnant longer than only one month." She said she had not had any sexual intercourse with her husband since the beginning of the year. And that this was a supernatural pregnancy and now she was carrying Yahweh's Holy Child. Her husband did not come, as he was sent back to the U.S. to a mental institution after he tried to strangle his wife in Israel. I heard later he was accusing her of adultery.

Sexual orgy

The handmaiden told me later that they and a Palestinian man, who was their taxi driver, had all been naked in one room touching each other and taking pictures. According to witnesses, this happened two days before the "Holy Conception". The lady told me much later that the Palestinian man had tried to come on top of her and have sex with her. She was expressing this as if she was surprised he would do such a thing. "What do you expect if you put a man with two naked women in one room and let him touch you and you touch him?" This ran through my head, but as always I didn't express my thoughts, otherwise I would be rebuked.

More stress

I had to learn to live in a messy house again and being controlled all the time. The lady had regular body manifestations which she called birth pain sessions. She was lying on the sofa and her body was jumping wildly up and down. Then we were all on the floor praying for her relief. I carefully stroked her face and she told me I had such a gentle hand and it helped her. Oh finally, I was scoring some good points. I wanted to have the same closeness that the handmaiden had with her, but it was very hard for me to come this close, as the lady acted much differently with me than she did with her handmaiden.

Many more birth pain sessions would follow after that. I learned that the handmaiden was also pleasing the lady sexually as God wanted to comfort her. She and the handmaiden were always together in the bedroom, and she was making videos for "The Last Call". Later she called her "her lady in waiting". The handmaiden was very strange to me and I still could not understand how she could leave her three daughters and husband behind just like that.

Though I took care of all the practical things, finances, website and supported them with all we had, I was never allowed to come closer to the lady.

Supernaturally fast

We saw that the lady's belly was growing very fast. She explained to us this was because it was a supernatural conception and therefore the baby was growing much faster than a normal pregnancy. This was going to be a short pregnancy she said.

At night they were taking pictures of her naked belly. They were also making food and eating during the night. Everything was contrary to our "normal" life. The lady said we were gluttonous because we were taking food on our plate for a second time, when we were still hungry. She said we were eating like pigs.

The farm lady

I was on my way to the farm with my bike. She was a really sweet humble woman that we knew for a while. It was a nice bike route through the woods and my husband and I loved to go over there. The farm lady and her husband had many cows and they made their own cheese, yoghurt and other things. They were not using any pesticides on their land. I loved to go in the stables and watch the young calves. She was always asking me about the ducks in the woods. "You can have this". Many times she gave me something extra for free. Then she packed the leftovers from the cheese. "This is for the ducks" she said.

The lady visited her last year in spring time and gave her a word from Jesus. The farm lady was, as far as we knew, not a born again Christian. She was all red in her face and looked ashamed when the lady "oracled" to her the love invitations from heaven. Even I felt ashamed. It reminded me of all the times when my mother spoke about her paranormal things to other people.

I opened the door from the little shop. "I haven't seen you for a while" she said. "We have been abroad but now we are back" I replied. I was buying milk and cheese for the lady. But we were not allowed to eat dairy, as this was activating our flesh too much, the lady said. The bread maker was also one of the items that we had to bring to recycle, as the bread was too strong for the flesh. No dairy, no meat or sugar was allowed, because this was feeding the demons in us. We had to stay on a moderated vegan Daniel fast. But the lady was eating organic meat and dairy for the baby in her womb.

Six armed police men

I opened the front door and I saw three armed police men on each side of the door. They all came in the house and were looking for the young lady who was with us in Cuenca. The lady had taught us that it was ok to lie if it was to protect her or anyone in the ministry. We just had to repent and Father would forgive us. We were also taught that we had to keep the lady very private, to protect her and the holy child in her womb.

"Who? What is her name? I don't know her." I said to the officers. The young lady's mother had been hiring private detectives to look for her. "And why is that lady running upstairs? Who is that?" They had seen the lady going upstairs to hide from the police. "Why is she not coming back? What is taking her so long?" they asked me. "She is changing her clothes" I responded. I continued to claim that I didn't know the young lady they were looking for.

Then the lady came downstairs with a big smile on her face. She acted very innocent asking the men if she could help them with something. "Oh yes, I know that young lady very well, she lives with us here in the house." I was looking at the lady and was thinking "What are you doing?" Didn't she know that I had just succeeded in convincing the police we did not know this young lady? The female officer looked at me and said "You are good, you are very good!" At that moment the young lady and the handmaiden came back from doing groceries. They took her to the police station and later she came back and all was well.

Mark of the beast

One of the neighbours told me that he tried to call me to warn me about the policemen at our door. He was worried as he thought these men came to force the mark of the beast on us. I had spoken to him earlier that this would come in the end times and that it was all part of the new world order system. Apparently, he had taken this very seriously. I could only imagine what the other neighbours were thinking about us. Hopefully no one else had seen anything.

The bathroom door

The soaking music was playing day and night and it made me feel depressed. I asked them to please turn the volume down a bit down at night so the neighbours would not be disturbed again. I could feel it was not ok for me to ask this. I felt stressed every time I wanted to say something and rehearsed the words in my head before I opened my mouth.

My husband and I had to wear a kippah on our head. So I had to remember to take it off every time I went outside, so the neighbours would not see it.

"Why is this bathroom door locked? No one is in there." I went on the roof to look through the bathroom window, but the room was empty. However the door was locked from the inside. Then I heard it was because of my sin. I worried how to pay our bills, since they used so much electricity and water. And I had asked them nicely to be mindful about this. The oven was on every day just to make the lady's crème brulee. The lights were on day and night in the house. No one bothered to turn them off. "The angels did this and now it is your fault that the children cannot take a bath for days!" she shouted at me. I felt terrible and I prayed hard to God to please open the door again. The door stayed locked for about a week. Then suddenly it was open again.

It reminded me of the past with my mother, when I was rebuked by the spirits and now I really thought that the lady could read my mind and thoughts. I just wanted them to leave and never come back again. I was already sinning again in my thoughts.

Strong rebuke
The lady was now sleeping in a separate bedroom by herself. The handmaiden was serving her food and coffee in her room. They bought a special bed table so she could eat easier.

I knocked on the door and opened the door to pass through, so I could go to our bedroom upstairs. The lady lay on her side in bed so I thought she was sleeping. "You are not trusting God for electricity bills and...." The lady was now sitting up in her bed and screaming at me so hard and loud that I surely thought the whole street could hear it. But she did not care, she gave me a full load with such anger that I thought for a minute she was going to hit me. Tears were streaming from her face and I was just shocked! I had not said anything else about paying bills or whatever. My husband and I just took care of it.

Why always naked?

Since we had to pass the lady's bedroom, my husband saw her many times sleeping naked in her bed. "Why is she doing that since she knows we can all see her?" I didn't understand it either, for me it was no problem but why could she not be more mindful towards my husband? Was she doing it on purpose? I thought we were all supposed to be pure and holy? These thoughts were inside me and I just couldn't help it. I was also still troubled because they took naked or half naked pictures at night.

Leaving

"You had better pray very hard and hope that you will be saved in the end. Right now it looks like you are going to hell! You will go through the worst persecution and torture. This is about your salvation now." All these words came out of her mouth towards me. "You don't even want us here!" she shouted while she went upstairs. I was nailed to the ground again. But I had to admit to myself that she was right and that I did not want them here. I never said anything to her about my emotions, I had always been very nice and serving her the best I could. I even tried to be her best friend! And I still did all the administration work to the best of my ability. Now I was really in trouble. I felt desperate and hopeless. Was I really going to end up like that?

Lost, and in hell? If there was anything in my life that I could not handle, it was that God was angry at me. And from the moment the lady came to our house, God had been angry at me all the time.

Fall 2013

"Why are you not led by the Spirit?" she shouted at the handmaiden, while they were loading up the car that we rented for them. They all left for Switzerland in a rental cottage, including the young lady who had been with us since the end of 2012. No one was talking to me anymore while I was helping to bring their things to the door. Despite the hard rebuke, I was still happy and very relieved that they were leaving, although I was hiding it, they knew it. "This is for you. I hope you take it seriously." The lady gave me a small paper with a scripture out of Jeremiah. It was a scripture of judgment. Those were her last words before they left.

CONSECRATION

Alone in the house again

My husband and I were alone in our house again. He was very moved about everything that happened and there was no room for rejoicing or slowing down. He encouraged me to really repent and get our deliverance. He said we came against the two witnesses and that was extremely serious.

After all this we could not relax anymore. We took it very seriously and separated ourselves, me in the office again and my husband upstairs. We hardly even went to the living room. I printed out all the scriptures about the heart and repented for every single one of them.

December 2013

My husband had to go to Switzerland with another rental car. Then he went with the lady and the others to the U.K. He was given a choice there: Follow the lady and thus fulfil his calling or come back to me in Belgium. He chose to follow the lady. I only found out about all this later, I had no idea what was going on. My husband was allowed to come back to Belgium to bring one of the rental cars back. But he passed his test as he chose the lady, his calling, and not me. When he told me that, I was very afraid and worried that it would happen again and that I would lose him. I was not ready to make that choice. The young lady also came back with my husband as she was rebuked by the lady and failed her test.

2014

We continued to consecrate ourselves in our rooms and prayed and repented every day. At some stage, I lost my new name. This spirit was now taken away from me and I had to earn her back. The new spirits given to us were also helping us to get our deliverance.

An email came for me. I was so happy to read that I had my new name back! My husband and I were always alert for any email. We analysed every word to make sure we understood things correctly. We were both so afraid to be rebuked or corrected. It brought us so much stress. Every time an email came with no rebuke, we were very relieved.

My husband was sad and disappointed though. He said he was not part of this ministry, as he had nothing to do. I, on the other hand, had a lot of work with the finances, administration and letters that had to be send out many times to ask for money. I was instructed that I could not discuss any financial matters with my husband, as he was worrying about it. Many times a word came from the lady that my husband had to make the right choice and trust God with the finances otherwise he could not be part of the ministry anymore.

March 16, 2014

I had to send out a Last Call letter to the email list to ask for financial help for the lady to help build her a church in Wales and to help her obtain the land and barn. Previously, we were traveling with the lady in Wales. The shofar was blown on this land. It was private property, but the lady said that God would buy this place for her, for the holy child to be born.

However this property was never bought by the lady and the donations she received were used for daily needs and food.

Annabelle

She was not as easy going as Hosea, but a real challenge. She raised her long neck and made it very clear that she was the boss. Annabelle was a beautiful Canadian goose that I trained in the woods. I was sure I could do the same with her as I did with Hosea. Annabelle had a friend that she abused all the time, but he loved her and followed her everywhere. I called him Spikkel. He was a musk duck.

"Come on Annabelle fly! You can do it! Come on! Fly!" Annabelle was running hard next to my bike on the grass trying to keep up with me and there she went, up in the air, her first little flight! Oh thank You Lord, this is so wonderful! I was so thrilled, this was really amazing wow. Annabelle never flew before. Her short flight ended abruptly as she had not learned yet to avoid trees. But she was fine and from that moment she could fly, which was so good to see.

She always came out of the water when she saw me. I fed her

butter cookies and grains. The next challenge was to be able to pet her on her back. She allowed me eventually, but in the beginning I had to endure some little bites. "Be careful of that one" the forester said to me. "She attacked me yesterday." I could not help laughing. I looked at Annabelle and said "How dare you!" I invited the forester to sit next to me on the bench and I fed Annabelle a cookie. "Now you do it" I said. Annabelle took the cookie out of his hand and ate it. I was hoping she would not bite him, but she behaved herself.

"What you do with those ducks and geese is amazing" he said. Then I had the opportunity to tell him the gospel. He didn't believe that God created all this beauty around him. He told me all kind of people come here, even a group of people that hug trees. I told him I do not hug trees. Then I thought, actually that would be nice to hug a big old tree!

No money

Although my husband was doing interim jobs in between, during summer time we had to get our food out of the big waste containers from the shops. My husband was brave enough to dig into the containers and get out what we could still eat. He brought lots of flowers also that were too old to be sold, but we put them everywhere in the house and in our rooms upstairs. The lady said looking for food in containers was all preparation for us for the end times.

July 23, 2014

I had to send out an urgent plea for financial help to the email list for the lady. They had been in 31 different places since the beginning of the year, in U.K., Wales, Scotland, Ireland and now again in the U.K.

October 2014 – Rebuke

A woman from the church came to our door. I was in the office and thought to just ignore her, as we were not allowed to have any contact with them. Then my husband opened the door and briefly talked with her. I just stayed in the office. But he did not invite her in.

The lady "oracled" at me and I got a very strong rebuke that I should not have opened the door and not have been so fearful. As a consequence I had to break my 80-day fast and I would not have any rewards for the 60 days that I already fasted. "I did not open the door, you opened the door!" I said to my husband. I was so confused and angry also, as we were suffering to get through this very intense fast, and we finally accomplished 60 days. However I humbled myself and repented for opening the door.

November 27 2014 – Friendship covenant

We were invited to celebrate thanksgiving with the lady in a cottage in Wales. We were there for only a few days. I was happy that we would not be stuck here and not able to go back home. The lady "oracled" so many words that there was hardly any time to eat. This time the words were good and encouraging.

The three of us, my husband, me and the handmaiden were all on our knees and on our faces, covered under our tallits. It was time for a special friendship covenant with God. She touched us with her special staff from Israel and prayed over us. Her hands were violently shaking when she was touching us. It was a special anointing coming upon us.

It was time to go back home. Wow, so now we were friends with God. This was a dream come true, because I always prayed to be God's friend. It was one of my hearts desires. I was surprised also how quickly things were changing, as only one month ago, I was rebuked so hard and lost all my rewards. God was so good and forgiving.

A baby

The handmaiden and I were told that at a certain time when Yahushua comes in the flesh for the lady, that the handmaiden and I would have the privilege to have sexual intercourse with Yahushua and that we would have His seed in us and carry His children. She said it would not be my husband's child but Yahushua's and that no one could know about this. My husband was heartbroken thinking he was not even worthy for me to carry his child. Later it was clear that only the lady was ordained as His bride and Queen.

My husband and I had the privilege to go on a trip once. We could go to a nice place at the sea in Belgium. We stayed there for one night and enjoyed different kinds of cheese with some wine. The lady prophesied that we would have a baby together named "Joshua". We would go to Switzerland to the nicest cottage where I would become pregnant. He would be part of God's army. We had a beautiful day and spent time at the sea and in the dunes.

Later the lady rebuked us for gluttony as we should not have eaten all the different things they served for breakfast.

2015 – Police interrogation

Our bank accounts were very active. Sometimes we were thousands below zero and sometimes there was a donation of thousands of Euros all at once. No matter what the situation was, we were trained to continue trusting God.

An officer came to the door and said that we needed to be interrogated for money laundering and fraud. The lady told us that she already knew that we were going to be tested this way, and so we could not say one word about her. My husband and I were sitting on the bus on our way to the police station. We were questioned separately with the same questions. The officer that questioned me was heartless and cold. He told me that he was a special investigation officer, like he was trying to impress me. I did not like him and he did not like me I guess. I was pretty relaxed and trusted God to get us through all this. After all, He would protect the lady.

The officer questioned me about all the different amounts coming into our accounts. These were all donations from abroad for the ministry. Many Asian people gave large amounts at once. I wondered what my husband would say, as he really did not know any details about the finances.
"So how do you decide where the monies go?" he asked me. "We pray and ask the Holy Spirit for guidance" I replied. He was so astounded by my response that he repeated my answer. "Yes that is right" I said. "Wow that is a special way of dealing with your finances" he said. He was clearly mocking me. I explained to him that we are Christians and that we pray about every decision we take. "Ok, so I am a pastor (*and then he said a random name*) from Africa and I send you an email with lots of pictures from the poor children I take care of. Oh, and I want you to send me the money by Western Union. You would send me the money right?" I replied that we would pray about it first. "And then you know what to do?" he asked. I said yes.

"Do you believe in God?" I asked the officer. "No I don't. And by the way you are not supposed to ask me any questions and I am not supposed to answer you!" I was looking at him and thinking, well then, why did you answer me? I was able to stay very calm and relaxed and answered all his questions with as much honesty as I could, without saying anything about the lady or the handmaiden.

"Well lady, I conclude that you are just very naïve." "I guess I am." I responded and lifted my shoulders in innocence. I was thinking, that is good, just let them think we are very stupid. The interrogation lasted for four hours straight. My husband told me that he got a young and very nice officer, as he was replacing the one who normally had to be on duty. He said he did not have to explain so much, since he told the officer that I was the one in charge and doing all the finances.

Wow, we passed a huge test! The officers were so nice to give us a lift back home. I could hear they were joking about poor pastors receiving money via Western Union. We never heard anything anymore about all this.

April 23, 2015
It was time to dissolve the non-profit organization YHWH-GLORY-END-TIME-MINISTRY. I was so relieved! We went to the notary, a very nice man in town. The lady met him in 2012 and gave him a word from God. Now I still had to finish everything for the accountant and I was done.

SELLING OUR HOUSE

Selling our house
The lady told us that we had to sell our house. The 144,000 could not have any properties. This was huge. "Are you very sure you want to do this? It is really not a wise idea." The man told us in the office who arranged our social loan. I didn't want to do it at all, we had such a good pay off plan.

This was another test of God and we had to obey and do it. "The mechanic will buy your house, you will see!" the lady said. I asked him and he said it was a good house, but he already had a house, so he was not interested in buying a second one. Then the lady said that we had to find something cheaper. So we started to look for an apartment, which I didn't like, but I wanted to show God I was willing to give up everything for Him. We didn't find anything cheaper than we were paying off for the house.

Then the lady said that we had to find a buyer that was willing to rent the house to us again. That was probably the biggest challenge. She told us to trust God and He would do this. We prayed and trusted God He would send someone.

Very soon a few couples came to see our house. They all wanted to buy it right away. But they did not want to rent it out. "Is there no one?" I asked the man from the estate office. "No one" he said, except this old man, but he always says he will buy houses, but he never does. He is always here. I don't take him seriously." "I want to meet with him" I said.

June 4, 2015 – Baby announcement
"We are ready to deliver our Man-Child, which was conceived after We prepared our Beloved K~ (name of the lady) and consummated with her in the Tabernacle she built for Us in Israel, in July of 2013. Heaven on Earth! Now, almost 2 years later, We are finally ready for Our Holy Child to be born."

The lady was asking for money in the letter to purchase all new furniture to set up her bedroom. Her missionary travels had added up to an estimated 30,000+ miles by car as she had resided in 67 different locations throughout the United Kingdom.

Rental contract

On June 5th, we signed our rental contract. The old man had bought our house. It was actually an investment for his son. I was so happy we could stay in this house. For us this was ideal, close to town, and yet the woods close by and a small garden that I could easily maintain. And the rental price was ideal too. We were blessed.

The lady told us we had to buy a car. She told us all the details. We found a nice car, too big for the two of us, but this was God's will. The rest of the money from the sale of our house was used by the lady. She spent it in almost a month. "God wanted it to be spent so quickly" she said. I thought "What a shame." I was never happy that we had to sell our house.

Wales – The three cottages

I was staying with the lady, the handmaiden and the children in rental cottages in Wales. My husband was in Belgium most of that time. I was very unhappy and so extremely lonely over there. We moved around in three big cottages, but on the same property. The owner was a nice elderly lady and I had to convince her that my husband and I were missionaries.

The cell-phone flew over my head and landed against the wall at full speed. The handmaiden had one of her angry moods. She said she went through so much deliverance and it was disturbing the lady. As always I tried to encourage her. During the day I had to take care of the two little children. Schooling them was always a challenge. They could only be outside for very short periods of time. Mostly they were put before the television to watch a Christian movie.

I was counting the hours. There was hardly any opportunity for me to just sit down and read my Bible. Every time I tried, the children were screaming or fighting and I had to get up again. Every cottage was the place where the holy child would be born. Every cottage was special, the lady said, and prepared beforehand. Yet we were always moving from one cottage to another.

"You have to move the Kuga in the garden behind the gate" said the handmaiden. "In that field behind the gate?" "Yes!" the handmaiden replied. She never took a lot of time to explain things to me, as she was mostly with the lady in her room, and the handmaiden could not spend too much time in my presence, or she would carry my demons into the room. I didn't understand this instruction, it sounded foolishness to me, but I did what I was asked to do. Why must the car be in that garden? I opened the heavy gate with much trouble and manoeuvred the car between the posts of the fence. In no time the car was stuck it was wider than the gate opening. I knew this would happen.

"What are you doing?" she yelled at me while she was running towards the car. I did what you asked me to do." NO! What are you thinking? You are not supposed to move the car in here, but over there!" The handmaiden stepped into the car and with much trouble and patience she was able to manoeuvre the car backwards until it was out of the very small spot.

Oh boy, I would probably hear it now. With heavy shoes I walked into the living room. The lady looked at me and said pretty calmly "This was totally the old woman. You have to fast more for your deliverance." I was surprised she did not scream at me. The handmaiden was always giving me my portions to eat, which were very small. I was never allowed to fix something myself or use the stove, and neither was my husband when he was around. I felt frustrated at times, because

111

we were treated as little children. There was hardly ever a compliment or a "thank you" towards us. We were treated as slaves.

"I feel Father wants me to tell you this. I am promoted now in heaven." I looked at the lady very interested in what she was going to say next. "Now I am learning and being trained to have sex with animals." I remembered she told us in the past that this was not a sin in heaven. I could not imagine how you even start with something like this. "And when He tells you to touch yourself then do it, even many times a day. Do everything he tells you to do." But what if I am deceived again, like in Cuenca, I was asking myself.

Sometimes the handmaiden and I were told that we had already been delivered from that Kundalini a long time ago, at other times we heard we still had the Kundalini spirit in us. Hope was given and then taken away. Nothing that was said was a certainty, as things could change any minute.

The lady bought a big fake phallus to prepare herself for Yahushua's coming. She said His phallus was big and so she had to be ready for that. The handmaiden was helping her in all that. She bought me sexy underwear and said my husband would really like this. I felt like a whore when I tried it on, and it was too small.

Pornography

My husband joined me in another rental cottage. I so longed for him every day and now he was finally here. The lady told us that we had to watch movies on the internet where people were doing tantric sex. This was also done in heaven she said and now we had to learn it too. I did not like it at all, neither did my husband. It just didn't feel beautiful and pure. It felt disgusting to me. She also bought me a fake phallus and other sexual tools for me and my husband to explore. Wow, heaven sure was totally different than I ever imagined. Apparently it was all about sex in heaven. The lady said that Father God had an appointment every day at the same time to have sex with Michael the archangel.

She taught us that everything that happened on earth with sexual pleasures was already in heaven. This also applied to all kinds of music on earth, amusement etc. Even rude language and words like "freaking" or "bullshit" are used in heaven by Father God. The lady said it was all created in heaven anyway. Therefore the lady started using expressions like "you better freaking repent" or "that is bullshit" or "God is pissed at you!"

The gang and preparing for Wales

Hope, Handsome, Hollie Wollie, Hope Junior, Fat One, Black Head. They were all still part of the gang. These ducks were so special to me, as God used them for all those years, so I could have some joy in between. We just heard from the lady that we had to move to Wales. We could keep our rental home in Belgium. It sounded similar to when we had to move to Cuenca. I sat on the bench at the pond. Hope and the gang were with me.

I prayed to God if He could please rapture these ducks up to Heaven, as I would worry too much when I had to leave them behind again. It was the end of June 2015 and little did I know what was going to happen next.

July 2015 –To Wales

"You need to come to Wales right away!" was the instruction from the lady. We arrived in a cottage and they had horses there. Oh how I longed to ride horses again one day... We stayed there for a month with the lady. I was so unhappy again, as we just stayed in the house day in day out, waiting for the lady to come out of her room, and then listening to her singing and "oracling". Around August we came back to Belgium.

They're all gone

"Come! Come! Hopie come!" no one came. The pond was empty. I knew something was very wrong and that I would see dead ducks in the bushes, if I would look for them. "Don't you know what happened?" a lady asked me. She explained that all the ducks suddenly died, "It went very fast" she said, "but they are all gone, and it is not the same anymore without the ducks..." Even she was sad.

I stumbled to the same bench where I sat in June. I knew they were dead. I had to know what happened. "Lord, what happened? Where are the ducks?" "Didn't you ask Me to take them all up to Heaven? I did, but I did it My way." "You seriously answered that prayer?" "Yes, I didn't want you to worry about them when you went to Wales." "Are they all gone? Did you take the whole gang?" "Yes the whole gang, not one is left." This was seriously one of the most amazing prayer requests I ever had answered, besides that one time when I prayed for a young goose that lost its eye, and the next day it was back with baby hairs growing around it.

I was sad, but happy at the same time. Now I would not worry about the ducks. Wow, I was going to miss my times with the Lord here in these woods. This was truly my secret place with Him.

HOPE

HANDSOME – HOPE – HOLLIE WOLLIE

HOPE

HOLLIE WOLLIE – HANDSOME

HOSEA

SPIKKEL--ANNABELLE

CHAPTER IV: WALES

WALES

September 2015

It was time to move to Wales for good. My husband's friend was going to take care of the mail, our house and garden. Now we knew why we had to buy that big car. The car never came back to Belgium. Wales was so different. It was always wet and raining, though the nature was very beautiful. I believe there were more sheep than men. We were living in a rental house from a Christian acquaintance with her two Indian boys. We had to take care of those two boys temporarily in cooperation with the mother. This was an instruction from the lady and she had arranged this with the mother.

My husband had to travel to Israel, He was there for about one month and I missed him so much. I thought he would never come back. Meanwhile I continued to work on the YHWH-GLORY-END-TIME-MINISTRY website as much as possible. One day, all my files were corrupted due to a virus. It had been a struggle from day one since March 2012 to work on this website. The lady said this was because it was Yahweh's website and thus it was attacked a lot by the enemy.

When my husband finally returned from Israel we bought a new bed as I needed a mattress that was more comfortable. The one I had been using was really hurting my back.

7 day Esther fast – Brexit

"Father is looking for one couple who is willing to do a 7 day Esther fast for Him." My husband and I were the chosen ones and so we agreed to do this. It had not been since September 2012 in Cuenca that we had last done a seven day Esther fast. It was very hot outside in Wales but we got through seven days without any water or food. "Thanks to your Esther fast David Cameron won the election with just two percent! Now Brexit will go through! Hallelujah!" My husband and I were praised for obeying God with this fast. Wow, we definitely scored good points with this one.

Judged

The white Ford Kuga had been leaking oil for a while. We could finally take it to a garage. However there was another problem that they noticed at the garage and it would cost £500. "They are trying to rip you off. That problem is not there, they are lying to you! They are judged! You can never go to that garage again." We continued to drive around with a car leaking oil. We kept a bottle of oil in the car and poured it in the oil reservoir regularly. We didn't understand why we could not just fix the car.

Moving around

We had travelled with the lady in several other houses and cottages previously where the holy child would be born. The shofar was blown and the property anointed, but these were not the places after all. Why were things not coming to pass as the lady had "oracled"? It was very stressful to move around with them.

One time I stayed in a nice house and I was rebuked and corrected by Yahushua the whole night for many hours. My husband was in Belgium at that time and I missed him. Why were we separated so much? That night I had to learn to sing and practise with the lady. My voice sounded terrible to me. "And He doesn't want to hear any more about your pains! He is tired of it" she said. I was shocked as I was not a complainer at all. In fact I was very hard on myself all those years since I had pain. So it surprised me greatly that God was tired of my complaining. Since then I never dared to show that I had pain anymore. I had to believe I was healed.

It was a long season again without my husband and I wish I could just talk to him about all this. I was instructed to throw away all my cushions, no more neck support while sitting down and also the medical seat cushion that I took everywhere had to go. The handmaiden and I drove to a place and we dumped it all into a private container. "Is it ok to dump this here? This is private property?" I asked her. But she didn't care.

Another cottage had a nice hiking trail nearby. Early in the morning while everyone was sleeping, I always went outside and walked this path. It was pretty steep and it cost me all my energy. I was thinking about what my husband was doing in Belgium. I wished I could go to Belgium. I did not want to return to the cottage. I was trying not to cry and did not dare to complain.

One cottage was very big and had a balcony from where you could see the dining room with the large table. The lady told us that she would stand on this balcony with the baby in her arms and Yahushua next to her. Wow, it had to be very soon now. We were excited that the waiting was almost over. Then it scared me also, because what would happen when the King would come and what would He say to us? Would He rebuke me or ignore me? I was troubled in my head with all these things. The lady was practising and was sitting on one of the royal red chairs. The long train of her wedding dress covered the chair.

No more Dutch
"God hates Dutch!" the lady said. From now on my husband

and I could not speak Dutch anymore, only English.

My husband and I were severely rebuked and threatened again that we would be separated in the end, one would make it, the other not. Every little bit of hope or enlightenment was taken away again.

"You can have a nice evening together and sleep in my bed that I used here. You two need the anointing." I don't want to sleep in the sheets that you used for the last week" I thought. There I go, sinning again. But I was very excited for a night with my husband, which was a unique opportunity. I prepared some vegan snacks. It was already after midnight when my husband came back. He had to help move the lady to another place. It was getting very late. He was frustrated because our night together was over and we had to get up early. "Then why does she say we can have a nice evening together?" he said in frustration. Hope was taken away again. Everything was used to break those old souls and we had to hold on to that and just continue on.

RENTAL CONTRACT

March 22, 2016

My husband and I signed a contract for a rental home in Wales. The lady found the house on the internet and we needed to rent it for her, because this was going to be the place where the holy child would be born. We probably will never go back to Belgium now anymore. I believed the lady was carrying a holy child, yet at the same time there was always a kind of inward resistance in me towards her, which I did not understand and could not explain.

Late nights

The boys had fallen asleep under their big tallits. We just finished another long session of listening to the lady singing and "oracling". It was time to go back to Burry Port. We all got in the car, grabbed our dry snacks, put on the worship music and left. This was one of our many trips back and forth that took us about one hour driving.

Sometimes for special occasions we joined a service in the chapel up the road. We all acted as one nice family. I was just crying inside because no one from these humble precious families had any idea what we had endured. We never tasted the pastries and other delicacies after the service. We just had a cup of tea.

Menu for the King

"What do you want to eat when the King comes?" I was looking at the handmaiden bewildered, not sure what she was asking me. She had a paper in her hand and we could all tell her what we would like to eat when Yahushua would arrive. That would be the menu. Oh wow, normally I was rebuked for thinking about food. Um, let's see, what would I want to eat? I am not sure. Maybe some cheese and oh yes a good chocolate cake! Ok, it was noted. It could not be much longer before the King would arrive, we had the house and the lady told us it was very soon now, so we had to be ready at all times.

Orders

"Amazon is here!" one of the children shouted. I quickly ran towards the gate to receive the packages. So much was delivered for the lady's preparation for the King. One day a beautiful Hampshire gold and cream couch was delivered. This had to be in the dining room together with the two golden thrones. Also special porcelain tableware and golden looking eating utensils were bought for the lady, which she used every day. We kept it separated from the things we were using. Also many prophetic paintings were delivered.

After so many deliveries, the delivery men started to complain and said they didn't want to come anymore with these big heavy packages. We needed to sign a special form. The handmaiden made a sign on the gate that said "All deliveries please in the black bin across the street." Several times a day we had to check the bin and empty it.

The glory is gone

The man from the office, responsible to check the house from time to time, came on the property. He went upstairs and quickly checked all the rooms. I stayed downstairs while he was doing his round. Once he left, I continued the work in the garden. The handmaiden ran out of the house and screamed at me "The glory left the house! This has never happened before! I never heard k~ (the lady) scream and cry like this! It's your fault, why did you allow that man to go in her bedroom all by himself? He touched and read her things and now the glory left! You need to leave the property right away!"

I was standing on the street totally dumbfounded and terrified. This was the worst thing that ever happened here. It is finished with me. I will go back to Belgium and suffer and go to hell. Afterwards I came back to Wales and all was well.

Druid

One day I had to get many tents that the lady bought second-hand. When I stepped into the man's house, I felt something strange. He then gave me a folder from him where it said he was a druid. The way he talked was creepy and I decided not to buy the tents. Many times we were tested also to see if we

123

would discern whether we should buy the things that the lady ordered or not. If people were smoking in the house, we could not buy it. So I believed I made the right choice here. The man was not happy, but I said it to him very friendly. I was severely rebuked when I came back without tents. The handmaiden had to go and buy the tents from the man and she apologized for my behaviour. The lady said the man saw I was totally manifesting the old woman. I felt so bad not having any discernment at all.

August 2016 – Second trip to Israel

I had been to Israel before to give money to a Palestinian man, the taxi driver who drove the lady everywhere in Israel back in 2012-2013. He had a Muslim background but believed in the lady and saw her as a prophetic fulfilment of the woman to come. This was the same man that was with the lady and handmaiden naked in one room in July 2013. The lady was supporting him financially from time to time.

Now, on my second visit to Israel, I was talking about my Christian faith and all of the sudden he started to kiss me all over my face (but not on my mouth). I did not kiss him back, I was totally surprised and felt paralyzed and he and I did not speak a word about this afterwards, nor did I tell this event to anyone else. But now I started to think about him.

Tenting

In September 2016 the lady told us we could finally move into our rental house with her. She had been living there for the last six months with the children and the handmaiden. Meanwhile they had changed everything in the house.

It became too much for the lady as she could not handle our deliverance, and we had to go tenting in the garden. The two

Indian boys were with my husband and I. Later, after at least six different camping places with ice on our tents because it was winter time, we were allowed to come back to the property.

It was so discouraging to hear about "the old woman" manifesting and "you're going through so much deliverance". It didn't matter if I was fasting or eating, I always heard these words.

The Gumtree trips – Accident

During the time from March 2016, when we rented the house for the lady, my husband spent much of his time doing trips to different people who sold their things. We called them "The Gumtree Trips". She bought pianos and organs, many decorations, lamps, furniture etc. One day a beautiful grand piano was delivered for the worship room. The handmaiden had to learn to play it and it sounded very beautiful.

I had to go to London again and stayed with the boys' mother. During that time the lady asked me to go and pick up a lamp that she bought from Gumtree. On my way back to the house in London I felt very sick. I had to throw up several times in the car. Luckily I had a bag at hand. I was driving on the highway and could not get off. It got so bad that I became unconscious for a few seconds. I woke up again with a big bang! I was covered with the airbags. The car was smoking and I saw the front panel of the car open.

I got out of the car and a man came to me and said I just hit his truck. A big truck was parked on the side of the road. There were many cars and they were moving very slowly. The truck only got a little damage at the back where one of the lights was broken off. He said the insurance of his company would pay for it.

The man was very friendly and I apologized. He asked me if he could do anything to help me and he called a vehicle recovery company. Meanwhile, I called the boys' mother and told her I had just ruined her car. She was very friendly and was only worried about me. My neck had taken a big blow. I felt so bad, as this was her brand new car. Fortunately it could be fixed. I wondered what sin I had done. Much later I heard it was because I had eaten cheese outside the fasting times, while we were supposed to stay vegan.

Another Accident – God's saving miracle

"You need to come back today" the lady told me over the phone. I was in London with the boys' mother to help her with some things. Later the handmaiden called me and said that I did not have to return that evening if I was not up to it, but that I could return in the morning instead. So I had the choice. I decided to go back that same evening anyway. When I was almost at Swansea, it was dark and I got very tired and decided to stop at a gas station and buy a coffee. I was hoping this was no sin and ok for God. I got back in the little grey car, a Ford KA, and was on my way again in the direction of Swansea.

The car was spinning around full speed over the highway. Oh no! I had fallen asleep. I grabbed the steering wheel. I hit the steel fence and then the car turned around like in a pirouette. I hit the trees on the other side. The car turned around full speed. "I am dying! I am going to hell! This is it." I hit the steel fence once more and saw a wheel coming off the car when it turned around in a pirouette again. I still held on to the steering wheel trying to bring the car straight again. Then the car stood still in the middle of the road.

The people in the car that I had seen from a distance behind me during all this, came running to me. "Are you ok?" "I am fine I just need a few minutes." It did not feel like I was hurt, only a little bit of blood on my face from a scratch. It was unbelievable that I was still alive and that the airbags not detonated. I had to be in major sin, why did this happen? I was terrified to even tell the lady. All of this ran through my mind while I was sitting there trying to comprehend what had just happened.

"You need to get out of the car" the man said. "Mam you need to get out of the car, it can explode any minute." I saw smoke coming out of the car and realized the fire department was there. I got out and they cooled the car. It did not explode. I saw that the front was totally destroyed. I just destroyed her car. What am I going to say to the lady?

Hard rebuke

An ambulance arrived and brought me to the hospital. "Hi, I just had an accident. I am in the hospital now." "You just had an accident?" the handmaiden repeated my question. She hung up and called me back after a few minutes. "It is because of your sin that this has happened because you did not listen to the Holy Spirit to stay overnight in London! You were only supposed to come back in the morning. I told you that very clearly, that is why I called you back in London. Michael the archangel spun the car. He did this to teach you a lesson and to put the terror of the Lord on you! He can do that perfectly! The lady already knew you were going to have this accident. And why are you in a hospital? You are fine. There is nothing wrong with you! Where is your faith? You don't need any examination. I am coming to pick you up."

I told the doctors I did not need any examination and waited for the handmaiden. We never spoke a word afterwards about what happened. The next days just continued on as usual. The car was totally destroyed. I did receive a letter later that the steel fence which divided the highway, was damaged and had to be restored. I called the insurance and luckily I was covered enough, so they paid for it.

February 5, 2017

Another Last Call Letter was sent out to the email list where the lady asked for help to get her ministry established on the rental property. *"And I shall establish an Operation now in two separate places in Wales where My Spirit shall pour out mightily when Eliyahu comes – MY SON WILL BE BORN! His Name is Eliyahu, My Son from the Womb of My Bride in My Hands. I say I shall establish two homesteads here with acreage, and many things I will do here, establishing an End-Time Tabernacle of Mine."*

The carpet

I had to travel to London again. I was so afraid to pass Swansea where I had that horrific accident. Now I was on my way to the centre to pick up a carpet. Driving in London is crazy especially when you do not know the way. I was at a huge roundabout and had no idea which direction to go. I prayed and asked the Lord to please help me. I took the easiest exit, and saw the name of the street which was the direction I needed. This was a miracle! I then found the address easily.

"I can't help you carry the carpet because I just had an operation in my back." I was thinking "You want to feel my back?" Eventually, the lady helped me anyway and we managed to push and pull the big Persian carpet into the Ford Kuga.

I was so thankful I got back in Wales safely. "And I will get that old woman out!" the lady shouted at me when I was in the kitchen. It was not a rebuke, or at least I did not think so, but more an encouragement from Father God that He would do it.

At least I had pleased Him with picking up that carpet in London.

Breaking the fast

The long fast was almost over and I was sneaking dry snacks upstairs in our bedroom. I paid for them with our Belgium money. My husband told me that we were going to be rebuked for this. But I was so tired of always being hungry and weak, working hard at the same time, and having to ask for a cracker like a little child. We took care of the house, the garden and did all the groceries. But we confessed about the food in our room and I was rebuked.

I really didn't like being here and I hoped everything was ok in the house in Belgium. I so longed to go back. Just to be able to breath and relax. How long was this going to last, until the holy child was born?

What a life? We were always rebuked but mostly me. My husband was mainly rebuked for doubt and fear. Several times a day, we had to do a long list of warfare prayers even at night.

SEPARATION

Separation

"You cannot pray for him anymore, nor even think about him anymore! If you do, you are in sin and then I will know." The lady said to me. I felt the same stress as in the past with my mother when I thought the spirits knew my every thought and emotion. It just felt this was even way worse. I had to let go of my husband completely. "God already has another man for you anyway and I have said that to your husband also. That is why I never see him in my visions at the end. I see only you." He was sent back to Belgium.

Now I was truly discouraged and heartbroken again. This whole walk all those years had been a roller coaster of emotions, from having a bit of hope to be together with my husband, and then hearing that God was separating us again. We also had heard many times we could not be together as the old people were manifesting too strong in us when we were with each other.

Many times I wondered what was left of our marriage. We were never allowed to do something together, celebrate our wedding anniversary nor birthdays, as that was giving food to the old ones. I was someone who liked to encourage other people and in the past I made sure I always had a nice card, a present or a surprise ready for my husband on those days.

However, we both did our very best to continue to serve the lady and take care of the house and garden. Also in Belgium, things had to be taken care of, and sometimes I had to go back for very short breaks for legal reasons.

April 2017

I was allowed to have a little break and travelled with the two Indian boys that were living with us to Spain. I know I was supposed to meet our landlord who lived there. But my husband could not go with us. I was surprised that they trusted me with such an important assignment. I prayed to God to please help me not to mess up this one. There was always one of us, my husband or I, who had to be at the property in Wales for the protection and help of our lady. After all, she and the handmaiden had been illegal in Europe for many years now, so they had to stay hidden.

We could stay in the apartment of the boys' parents. The boys and I had a great time and we always had something planned for every day. I made sure they had their fun. It was so great to be out of the "lockdown" in the house in Wales and just be "free" in Spain.

April 16: "I really think it's him. He is watching us, let's go back and see if he comes to us." With open arms and a smile a big man with long curly grey hair came towards us. I was buried into his arms and received a big hug. Wow, this was the landlord? He is great! I love this man!

"Order whatever you like" he said. The menu looked great, but I stuck with a pasta vegetarian, as we could only eat Daniel food. We had such a great time and it clicked so well between the man and I. He was more like a father type to me. Of course we were careful not to say anything about the lady in his house in Wales. I just had to make a good impression on him. I felt bad because I was cheating on a man who had been nothing but good to us all those years. But our test was always not to say anything about the lady and her child in the womb. That was top secret. I spoke with the lady and told her how wonderful the meeting went with the landlord. She was very pleased.

Late nights

At times we were all together sitting outside in the evening till late at night. I was frozen but patiently listened to the lady's talking, singing and "oracling" hoping it would end soon. I hated being here. I hated this life. But each time I encouraged myself that this was all necessary for our deliverance and purification and it was just a very narrow path we had to walk and it felt uncomfortable. So deal with it! And who else had the privilege to sit with the Queen and only Bride of Yahushua?

This was also all preparation for the King's coming to the property. The lady said that the King would come from heaven on a big white elephant and she showed us the exact place in the garden where he would pass. I always wondered how that would be and if we would see it. Though now I was disappointed that He would not come on His big white stallion.

We also had to bow before the lady when we came in her presence and when we left. For some reason this was hard for me to do. My bowing was probably the worst of all.

I believed in the lady and did everything for her, yet there was always that resistance that kept me from truly surrendering in my spirit like the handmaiden did. I believed that was the old woman manifesting like she always said.

THE BARN

May 31, 2017
My husband and I signed the new contract. The neighbours next door had moved out and the lady told us we had to rent this place too. Now we had the whole property and we had to trust the Lord for monthly donations. The lady called the neighbour woman a witch and said that God would take her out.

"It is your fault that the devil came on the property!" she screamed at me. I was looking bewildered at the lady. We were outside in the garden. "That old woman was really manifesting, you are going back to Belgium!" God was so angry at me again, because the previous renter of the barn had come on the property and she wanted to take pictures, which we did not allow. We were cleaning the barn but she probably did not know that we were the ones renting it now.

Many times the lady told me or my husband, whoever was

rebuked, that we would be rounded up in Belgium and would suffer in the camps.

Belgium

I repented for manifesting the old woman so much. I hated those words and wondered when I would finally receive my deliverance. During every separation from my husband, I was not allowed to contact him, no emails and no phone calls. It was hard to relax, as guilt was upon me with every move I made. I had to make sure I was not eating too much and to keep fasting.

Annabelle had left the woods. Good thing she could fly now. She was gone already after the first time I came back to Belgium. The pond was empty and so different. I felt lonely and sad.

Meanwhile my husband was in Wales and painting the barn and putting in new carpet. He too wanted to please the lady as much as possible. Though he was rebuked by the lady, as she said he was not supposed to put in the carpet, it had to be done by a professional.

We had to take turns. When I went back to Wales, he came back to Belgium and visa-versa, so we hardly saw each other anymore. Most of the time, my husband was working interim jobs whenever he was in Belgium.

Flat tires

We had so many flat tyres, that we kept a tyre pump in the car. This night my husband and I were sitting in the car. He had to take me to the bus station as I was returning to Belgium. Only a few minutes after we left we had a flat tyre. We did not even have a tool to put a new tyre on. We were always dependent on other people to help us on the road.

One night I had to bring my husband to the bus station as he was leaving for Belgium. It broke my heart every time we had to say our goodbyes. We hardly dared to hug or give a kiss, as we had to keep our distance from each other. I was always so stressed out when I was all alone on this small road on the mountain while it was pitch dark.

In the barn

My husband moved the bed that we bought in 2015 into our room in the barn. We had the smallest room, but our things just fitted in. I was so happy that my husband and I could now live in the barn with the two boys. Finally, we had a bit more freedom and privacy. However we were not together much, since one of us was mostly in Belgium. We were told that the old people in us were manifesting too strong when we were together.

Every day we took the boys to college. I hope the lady is not watching me. I quickly stepped in the car on my daily escape to school, hoping the lady would not see us from her bedroom window. The lady and the handmaiden still lived in the white house. She had two bedrooms, the biggest one with a large king size bed and "the white bedroom" as she called it, prepared for the King to come.

She had bought the furniture in the barn from Gumtree, an online ad where you can buy and sell second hand things. The boys received a huge pool table that they did not really want and hardly used. The lady just picked everything out and my husband had to go pick it up. The boys were opening up to me more now and said that they wished they could choose themselves how to decorate their bedroom. But none of us had a free will.

Some furniture was so big that it was a struggle to get them into the barn. My husband was rebuked hard because a little damage occurred on some of the things whilst moving the furniture. It was like we were always set up for rebukes.

The mower

She is probably watching me. Smoke came out of the machine. The riding mower broke down again. I had to go in the house and tell the handmaiden. Of course it was my sin. Every time something broke down in the house, it was mostly my sin. "The grass is too long, we should not wait that long before cutting it" I said gently in a rare bold move. "Father knows best and He decides when the grass will be cut, it is because of your sin that it broke down!" Even my husband was frustrated about this as he knew this riding mower was running on gas and made to cut short grass. But we had to wait till the grass was long and then the belts of the machine could not handle the long grass and thus the belts broke down every time again.

Since we had to wait too long, it was a big work to rake all the grass together and bring it to the field at the other side of the road. This work was so hard for me. Though my back was much better than before, and I believed this was God's mercy on me. The landlord told us he never had to rake the grass as he was cutting it every week, so raking was not necessary. I wished we were allowed to do this. It would have made it so much easier and much less work. For some reason, we had to do things contrary here and it made things complicated and brought us into problems.

I finally finished all the raking and did it pretty fast. Also the field across the street was a huge job, it was very steep and it took all my energy just to do that field. "Next time you need to do it in two hours, mowing and raking" the lady said. I thought that was impossible and the Lord knows that was impossible. I kept doing it at the same rate and she never said anything more about it.

The roses

I made sure the garden always looked perfect. There was a rose bed and it was in the form of a heart. When the lady looked down from her white bedroom, she saw a big heart. So I had to be careful to keep it in that shape. The lady always came to check the work I had done and I always hoped she was pleased.

Alcohol

There were still many bottles of alcohol in the kitchen cabinet from the previous occupant. The bottles were opened and alcohol was disappearing. In the end, the lady told my husband that I drank them but that I refused to confess it. I couldn't believe she said that, as alcohol makes me sick and I never drink it, as I never had any desire for alcohol. My husband pleaded with me to just confess it, but I refused as I did not drink it.

The Palestinian man visits Wales

The Palestinian man was invited to visit the lady in Wales. We were all in the worship room listening to the lady who was singing. I tried to convince my husband to come sit next to me on the couch, but he refused. The Palestinian man heard it and grabbed me, threw me down on the sofa and said "If you don't want her, I will take her!" This all only lasted for a few seconds and it seemed no one had even noticed it.

In the following days the handmaiden told me that she had to massage the Palestinian man's shoulder. Then the lady instructed her to go upstairs and make love with him. When I heard that, I was shocked. The handmaiden explained to me that as long as the seed does not go into her, she does not consider it as making love. Perhaps this was also how she saw it with the young man in Cuenca?

Black clothes

We were instructed to only wear black clothes from the moment we returned from Cuenca in November 2012. We had to renew them after a few seasons and throw the old ones away because they became too saturated with my deliverance. The lady would feel this deliverance and that could hurt her or the baby. So when we were invited in the lady's room or in her presence to worship, we had to take a shower, wash our hair and wear white clothes. We kept these separated so they would not be defiled.

Sometimes when I was in Belgium, I took advantage of the opportunity to buy some new clothes, the cheapest I could find. Normally I had to ask for everything in advance, but I never received any new clothes in Wales, so I bought them here in Belgium, where I could easily find them.

My back was hurting so much from looking around in the shops to find the best deals. I also needed a warm winter jacket and shoes. I was always so cold in the house in Wales, and I felt God was blessing me by finding some nice warm things. In Wales my clothes were often dirty from working in the garden, so it would be good to just have a second jacket for when I had to go out for shopping. I was hoping people would not notice that I was always wearing the same dirty clothes. Luckily in Wales people are very humble and simple, so they don't really check you out.

"You were not supposed to buy those! God was already telling me that you were having a good time in Belgium, going out shopping. You even went to a restaurant! You have not done what you were supposed to do, staying consecrated and repenting. Oh yes you repented, but not as you should have done. You were totally the old woman!!" But I never went to a restaurant, I was thinking. Why is she saying that? I had to hand over everything I had bought, even my warm socks. We will give these to the young lady when she comes.

They were referring to a young lady that was instructed to come to Wales from the U.S. I had no warm clothes for the winter. I noticed that the handmaiden was wearing some of the clothes that I bought. Why was she always privileged with new clean clothes but never my husband or I?

The young lady

I had to go and pick her up at the airport near London. I spent the whole day waiting in the arrivals hall and talking to the authorities over the phone. They refused to let her into the country and so she had to go back to the U.S. right away. I never saw her, although she was just one door away from me. "She was not ready. Too much deliverance" the lady said. But didn't God know that? Then why did she come and make that long trip over the ocean? Not to mention the waste of money. Thoughts that I probably was not allowed to think went through my head again. Later I heard the authorities sent her back because she had no return ticket. Why did the lady not know she needed a return ticket? Then there would not have been any problem for her to enter the U.K. The lady told us it was a just a test for the young lady.

June 2017

The lady said we had to sell our white car, the Ford Kuga that we bought in Belgium after we sold our house. I had to drive it to London and try to sell it there. Meanwhile, I was staying with a Christian acquaintance. The car looked brand new. I did not understand why we had to sell it now. I put an advert online and was trusting God it would be sold quickly. After a few weeks, the car was still not sold and I had to return to Wales. "It was just a test for you" the lady said. "To see if you would give up your car?" I was thinking, of course I would but surely God knew that already beforehand. Anyway, I was glad I passed my test.

Summer 2017 – Chatting

During the summer of 2017, the Palestinian man started to chat with me. He expressed in a very clear way his desires towards me. I was very surprised about this revelation but I was flattered and happy that he felt this way about me. I responded back to him that I felt the same way and the fire was stirred up in us right away. I was very discouraged in my marriage, at the point of being desperate and hopeless, and so I gave in into this sin, which was of course no excuse. But I was charmed by this man and to be honest, these chats, although they were very short, were such a pleasant refreshment in between all the hard rebukes and constant stress and fear all those years, that I really did not care right now. My flesh took a hold on me and it gave in to this excitement and new hope of "just being loved". He told me that he made love with the handmaiden when he visited us in the house, but that he had totally forgotten about her.

I was alone in the house in Wales as the lady had left for Scotland and my husband was camping with the boys.

Fasting

During all this time we continued on with our weekly Esther fast. It had been reduced to two days for some time now. But we had to do the big yearly fasts on January 1st for 60 days,

139

April 1st for 40 days, July 1st for 21 days, and September 1st for 60 days, which eventually became a 100-day fast. We were always eating vegan. Only the lady was eating organic meat from farms, fish and dairy from farms, because the baby needed it she said. Everything had to be the best for her.

SCOTLAND

Summer 2017 – Scotland

The lady, the children and the handmaiden had moved to Scotland. She did not feel safe anymore and they left Wales for a season. There was always some kind of drama going on. I often wondered if the enemy was organizing this to put extra stress on us. I had to drive every week to Scotland to bring the lady and her household more things. Now I was allowed to go in her bedroom and take her personal things that she requested. "It will probably be defiled when I touch it." I was thinking.

Fortunately I could use the comfortable Ford Kuga. The trip lasted for 12 hours and I only took one short break to go to the bathroom and check the oil level. The leak had still not been fixed since 2015. I added some extra oil just to be sure. I could not use GPS for navigation guidance. I had to learn to listen to the Spirit. I could only use a map, but I could not read the map as my eye sight was too bad.

I printed out the route on Google maps. That helped me to get on the correct main roads. But once in the wilderness of Scotland I had to find my way led by the Spirit. I thought there would be no end to this wilderness. Not one house, not one human being. It was getting dark and I wanted to be there before night. It was scary but I put on the worship music in the car and prayed for protection. All of a sudden a deer ran over the small road and hit the lights while trying to jump over the car. "No!" I was screaming. I stood on the brakes and I prayed immediately for the deer not to be wounded. I got out of the car and looked around, but I saw no deer. I was hoping it was ok and not hurt.

My heart went back to normal rate and I continued my journey. Now it was pitch-dark. Not one light on these small roads in the middle of the mountain. Oh please God help me. I came to a small intersection and had no idea which way to go. I went straight ahead. Am I really on the right road? "Yes you are, continue onward." I heard in my spirit. I asked this question many times and I kept hearing the same answer.

I finally saw one house and I parked on the driveway. It was dark and empty. This was not the place. I quickly got back in the car and locked all the doors from the inside. I continued to follow the small road in the middle of nowhere. Yes! Oh I was so happy when I saw that familiar black Range Rover. I found it! I opened the gate and parked the car backwards in the small spot on the driveway.

"Hi, oh good you made it! But we have to do warfare soon." Ok. I unloaded the car and then we did warfare together. I secretly grabbed some more crackers out of the car as I was so hungry. I lay down for one or two hours in the sofa, but could not sleep, as it was too uncomfortable. Early in the morning before 5am, I went to the kitchen hoping to have some breakfast before taking off again to Wales. I wanted to leave early so I would be back before dark. "Are you hungry? Do you need something before you go back?" the handmaiden asked. "That would be good, yes thank you." I only had some Jacob crackers in the car the previous day on my way to Scotland. It surprised me that they thought I could just survive and function without food most of the time. Apparently they were never hungry.

Mid August 2017 – Michael the archangel

I asked the handmaiden how she was doing. She told me things were hard as Michael the archangel was training her now through the lady. He was taking over her vessel and these rebukes were even much harder than the ones she received from "Wisdom". I always tried to encourage the handmaiden. Although I could not cope with her very well as she was such a strange being and she was always hard and indifferent to me. I still had compassion for her and told her that God was seeing her heart and all the sacrifices and surrender day and night that she was offering him, to serve the lady.

At times I had to follow them with my car when they were moving to a new place in Scotland. Both cars were fully loaded, and they had the children with them. Miraculously, I always found my way back to Wales safely.

During this time my husband and I received an instruction from the lady that we had to go together to Scotland for the weekend. The lady "oracled" to both of us but mainly it was my husband who was rebuked this time and he was told God had another man for me if he would not change. I told the lady when my husband was out of the room that I believed God had indeed another man for me, having the Palestinian in mind, and that I asked Him to confirm it through her. The lady was smiling at me as to confirm that the new man would really come in my life.

She also told us many times that God told her everything about us, especially if there was any sin, and for sure God had told her about the chats between me and the Palestinian man. Yet she never rebuked me for it, nor mentioned anything, she was even quite friendly to me now. This had been one of the greatest confirmations for me that it was indeed God's will for the

Palestinian and I eventually to be together, once we were taken up and glorified.

The trip back to Wales was terrible. My husband was driving and lost the way. It took us many extra hours to find our way back to the highway that led us to Wales. All the confusion caused a lot of stress and strife between him and I in the car.

Every time, when there seemed to be a little bit of hope and light at the end of the tunnel, we were severely rebuked or some drama happened. This was one of those days. I truly hated this life with the lady, and wished my husband and I could just be together in Belgium. At least in the past I was witnessing to lots of people. Now during all those years, we had done no witnessing at all, except trying to convince a few people we met on our way, that we were missionaries from Belgium in the U.K.

End of August 2017, my husband had to go to Belgium very briefly. Once he was back, I had to return to Belgium.

The 144,000

I also wondered many times how my husband and I could stand together as the 144,000 if he was so depressed and fearful. All this and the lady's visions about us not being together in the end, led me to believe that the Palestinian was going to be my partner in the 144,000. And I could only be happy for my husband that at least he would not have to be here on earth during the tribulation and die as a martyr.

The lady taught us that the 144,000 would be taken up to a special place and be trained, then paired two by two and send back to earth, to help many in the tribulation. Our bodies would be changed, so we would not be hungry or sleepy or tired and no one would be able to touch us. This was the great army as described in the Bible. This sounded great! However we all would die for our faith in the end as martyrs. And since we were trained for the highest ranking at the top of God's army, we were going to die like the two witnesses: crucified on a cross in Israel. We had the benefit to live with the lady and the other witness, the holy child, but we would also suffer with her at the end. That would be the last great test.

September 2017 – Moving back to Wales

The lady was moving back to Wales. I drove to Scotland and helped the handmaiden packing the white Kuga and the black Range Rover and followed them on the way back. It was so hard to follow them, and I could not see anything through the back windows as the car was fully packed. They drove so fast! A big truck trumpeted very loud and my heart stood still. I barely missed this truck and I wondered how it was even possible. I knew God saved me here from a huge disaster. There was so much traffic on the roundabout that I lost the black Range Rover once I was on the main road again. I was frustrated and anxious because they were not waiting for me. I had to continue on without them.

I was back in Wales and almost home. I felt the car was losing power and I drove down a small country road where the car dropped dead. I was in much trouble again. The car had to be picked up by a mechanic. He told me how lucky I was this did not happen on the highway. The Lord once again had saved me from a severe accident.

Another cottage

The lady was now in Wales renting another cottage. The Lord Yahushua spoke through her and cried to please reconcile with my husband. It was really time now! I felt so humble because she was not shouting this time. The car broke down because of the strife between my husband and I she said. I was confused because so many times she had told us that we could not be together any more, not pray for each other etc. And not so long ago in Scotland she confirmed to me with that smile that I would have another man. Was I now going to be together with my husband or with someone else?

I also knew I was in major sin with the Palestinian man by keeping quiet so long about what happened back in Israel in 2016 and the chatting periods after that.

September 2017 – The boys
In September 2017, the parents of the two Indian boys wanted them to come back home. My husband called me in Belgium and was very upset. The lady said it was my husband and my fault that this had happened, because we were striving with each other and not loving as we should. How could we love each other? There was never an opportunity. And when we were together in brief moments, we had so much stress and fear that it was very hard to even relax with each other. Besides, we heard all the time that we would be separated in the end anyway.

I repent, Lord please forgive me for being so rebellious. I know I have not been a good wife. Now the boys are leaving because of me. I felt terrible and full of guilt, also because of the Palestinian man and I. Was it because of this sin that the boys were leaving?

Fall 2017 – Back in Belgium
The lady came back to the white house. I was rebuked because the office was totally defiled and also the pillow I had used on the chair. Was this because I had been chatting with the Palestinian in this office? I was also rebuked for other things in the house and I heard that this was all a test for me to see if I

could take care of the house by myself. I had failed miserably.

When I was back in Belgium, I told the Palestinian man that what we were doing was "sin". I also wanted to see how he would respond to that. Perhaps he was wrong in his revelations about him and I? He said no it is not sin, but the sin was the wrong seed and that my husband had the wrong bloodline. He also said this was my "Last Call" and that I had to obey God in this. He seemed upset as I really did not understand his explanation. He told me how the Spirit had showed him many visions about me, confirming to him over and over again, and that he was dreaming about me every night, and when I would come to Israel soon, then it would be time for us to be together.

This was exactly what the lady also told me already, that my husband had the wrong seed. I wondered if this was the new man that God had for me. I felt bad for my husband, what was going to happen to him in the end? Was he still going to Heaven? I prayed to God to please bring my husband to Heaven when it was time, so he could be happy and safe. He had expressed many times to me that the only thing he wanted to do was to leave this earth and go to Heaven.

The man asked me several times when I would come to Israel, but I explained to him that I do not make these decisions, and could only come when the Lord would tell the lady. I told him several times we should be honest to the lady and tell her what was going on. But he kept saying no, that the Lord would tell her Himself, and he said for me to trust God. I thought ok, maybe he knows better. I was so overwhelmed and confused, fearful and scared, but at the same time happy and joyful that a man, like him, could love me or even want me.

He told me that he had been in consecration in the desert,

repenting for us, and that God was very angry at me. I asked him why? What did the Lord tell him? He said God was very angry at me because I asked him earlier to tell the lady about us and the desire for me going back to Jerusalem. I truly did not understand this reaction but I repented anyway for asking him that question earlier. I was very fearful of God and I believed the Palestinian heard from God. The lady was always talking good words about him and he was fasting so much and consecrating himself.

The man talked how he was now in even more debt because the lady told him that she would pay for his children's schooling. However, once he signed the school papers, she did not give him any money. Then he was obligated to get another loan with the bank and he was very angry at the lady. I was confused about this situation and didn't really know what happened.

October 2017

My husband and I were severely rebuked by an oracle from the lady. She rebuked us in the name of Yahweh, and she said we had 30 days to get our marriage back in order. This was our LAST CALL. It was so severe that we both thought we would get kicked out of the ministry, and we were sent back to Belgium to repair our marriage.

Later the lady said that the boys left the house because there was too much deliverance coming from them and they just had to go, and this was God's doing. I felt a bit more relieved when I heard that, but then why were we blamed first? So often it was like this, we were blamed for something, and then later another reason was given.

Milk and traffic

I had to go to a farm to buy some milk for the lady. The place was very hard for me to find, but I managed anyway. On my way back, I got stuck in the traffic. Hours went by before the cars started to move again. When I was finally back, the lady told me this happened because of sin.

Kenneth Hagin Senior

It was one of those nights. The handmaiden and I were sitting in the worship room on the floor. We were rebuked the whole night by the lady who seemed to sit very comfortable all night in her sofa with her legs crossed. I pushed the arm of the handmaiden who had fallen asleep. "Wake up, she is still speaking."

"Look at me!" the lady said. We heard that we both failed as a prophet. I was reduced to an evangelist now. An angry voice talked through the lady at me and was not pleased at all. It was humiliating and I felt everything I tried to build up the last years with the Lord, was a joke. It seemed I was standing nowhere yet. "This is Kenneth Hagin" the voice said. Oh wow Kenneth. I liked this man, I listened to his teachings sometimes, but he had passed away in 2003. Now I did not like him anymore. Why is he so mean now while he is in Heaven? He told me I had to pray every day three hours in the spirit and one hour before I got up out of bed. This nightly rebuke lasted for 12 hours. Many times I had to fight not to fall asleep and keep my eyes fixed on the lady. I wondered how the lady could stay so energized. I was in such pain from sitting on the floor all that time, though it was carpet, it still hurt.

Attack?

The next day the lady was all dressed up in the dining room. Her little boy was going to anoint her. He was her little prophet now. I heard her say everything and he had to repeat it. Many times he only spoke half of the words as he did not know them.

Later I heard, while I stood in the hallway as the ceremony took place, that the old woman in me tried to strangle the lady. I was thinking, but how did that happen? I was just standing there. I was a danger for the lady and her baby and I felt terrible about that.

Wood

New firewood was delivered. We kept several bags under the tarp on the field across the street. My husband was in Wales and he decided to ask the farmer, who always helped us to put the big heavy bags on their place, to bring several bags up to the barn, where he stacked it under a covering. This was much better as we had to go get wood daily in colder days. My husband then got rebuked by the lady and he had to bring it all back to the field. She said the farmer was not allowed to come on the property. Though it only took a few minutes for him with his machine. My husband moved all the wood back with a wheel barrow bit by bit. This was so ridiculous; yet another thing on the list that did not make sense.

2018 – The caravan

My husband had to bring the caravan we just bought for the lady, to the property in Wales. I was in Belgium and he told me that the white Ford Kuga was all smoking and it hardly managed to pull it on the steep driveway. We never travelled with the caravan. It was on the property all that time. Later, I had to put an advert online to sell it. But it was never sold, as the lady wanted to have more money for it than potential buyers offered.

Spring time

I had to go back to Wales and my husband had to work in Belgium to earn money for the lady. I had to be in Wales as painters were coming to scrape and sand down the external wall from the white house, and then put two coats of white paint on it.

It was always a drama when outsiders came to the house. I had to look for different people and then decide which one would be good or pure enough to come. "They cannot smoke on the property. You need to tell them to go across the street." I asked the lady if I could serve the two men some cookies and coffee, and she said "Yes that is fine to give them some cookies and coffee." I just wanted to be polite and they were very nice. The man talked about his girlfriend about to give birth. I told them my husband and I were Christians and gave a little testimony. "You were not supposed to give them cookies and coffee! Father is not pleased with that. This is the two witness ministry and here they need to work! Full time!" the handmaiden said. "But the lady told me that I could give them cookies and coffee!" "No she did not, you need to repent." There was always a reason for rebuke.

"They are judged!!" the lady said. "They will see what happens with their new-born baby!" The lady judged the baby to death. She said the man was in sin. I was shocked again to hear this. At times I did not know what to think anymore of all this. Why was God so mean and always angry? Is there anyone on this earth besides the lady that is pleasing to Him?

Mower broke

"Oh no. NO!" I was stuck again in the grass with the riding mower. The key turned around and around. There was something wrong with the lock. The machine would not move or start anymore. I covered it as good as I could to protect it from rain and two men from the shop came to have a look. They said it needed a new lock. So they put in a new lock. Then the machine worked again.

"You two need to go around the property and anoint it with oil and the blood of Yahushua", which was grape juice we used. "Those men defiled the garden and property with their demons! No one is ever going to walk in my garden anymore to defile it!" the lady said very angry. I could not help to think, what about me then? Do I need to stop doing the gardening work? The handmaiden and I went around and prayed and put the anointing oil and blood of Yahushua around the property.

Walking on eggs

I was walking on eggs; I hardly dared to breathe anymore in her presence, what a stress.

June 2018 – Back to Wales

Every time I came back from Belgium I would meet the lady, it was like a check-up to see if I had received enough deliverance from the old woman. It reminded me of that time when the neighbours and my mother came to pick me up in the Catholic building, expecting to see a total transformation in me.

At arrival, I could have a look in the barn and it was totally transformed. Coloured curtains were beautifying all the windows and lots of fake garlands and flowers decorated the rooms, many of which hung on the ceiling, which was not my style. The lady had moved into the barn using the biggest bedroom. The handmaiden used our bedroom now. The barn will be dirty and stinky in no time, I thought. During the day the lady spent time in the white house.

The handmaiden had her hands full running back and forth every day with all the cushions and blankets. When the lady was sitting somewhere, everything had to be covered with her blankets. She could not even sit on any chairs we were using, as these had too much deliverance. Also all the kitchen stuff for making meals for the lady had to be moved back and forth all the time, depending on which house she was in.

Tenting

Because of all the deliverance I went through, I had to sleep in a small tent in the garden, hidden between the trees, so it would not be noticeable to people in the street. I found my things in cardboard boxes in the loft and some things that had too much deliverance were put in the shed in the field across the street. I had to throw that all away as it rained in the shed and the stuff got all mouldy and was used by mice for nesting material.

Every morning at the same time, my little tent was filled with an orchestra of birds singing their praises which was amazing and exceptionally beautiful.

I tried to avoid the lady, as I felt stressed every time she came near to me. I was afraid she would feel my deliverance and I did not want to manifest the old woman in her presence. I was "hiding" in the laundry room early morning when she was passing by to go back to the barn. "Is she gone now?" I asked the handmaiden. "Yes it is fine you can come out now she is gone." Whenever the lady was resting in the barn, I cleaned the white house. It still surprised me how messy it was every time.

I felt so uncomfortable and uneasy, I was there at the property to do a lot of work, yet I had to hide as much as possible. Whenever the lady talked to me, I was stressing inside because I never knew what she would say and I also wanted to make such a good impression, acting as the new spirit, and hoping nothing of the old woman would be visible.

Good words

"Come in!" she said. I took off my shoes, and went into the

barn. To my surprise I could take a seat and sit close to her. I was already uncomfortable thinking that I would defile the place. She gave me good words and I wondered why she did not say anything about me and the Palestinian man. It was obvious she did not know yet. Why did God not tell her? She praised me for never complaining traveling back and forth and that this had been a huge test for me.

"Father wants you to be more comfortable" the lady said. The handmaiden and I moved a heavy sofa from the shed in the field, to put in the little tent. The sofa was even more uncomfortable than the inflatable mattress I had used, as the sofa was so short and now I could not even stretch my legs anymore, unless I put them on the high armrests, so I was forced to stay on my side all curled up. I did not dare to say anything to the lady about this, as I did not want to appear ungrateful.

Back to Belgium

There was a huge storm and the water poured into my little tent. Even my big suitcase that filled half of the space was under water. I wrung out my clothes with my hands as much as possible and dried them outside on chairs and tables. "Oh that is a sign from God that it's time for you to go back to Belgium." I was so happy to hear this! Fortunately the sun was shining so my things dried pretty well.

CHAPTER V: MORE REBUKES

THE ACCIDENT

July 5, 2018 – Tragic accident

"You have to come right away! She cannot walk anymore, it's really bad. The bone is sticking out of her leg!" Oh no, what happened now? "She was pushed by an invisible force and she fell forwards while she was worshiping at the chapel in the garden. I cannot do all this work by myself." The handmaiden was in a panic. Then she let me know that it was not necessary for me to come after all, because Father was doing a miracle in her foot and leg. I was so relieved to hear that.

However my husband had to return to Wales for a short time. The lady was in a lot of pain and could not walk. She was staying in her bed in the white house. She got a revelation that evil men were doing a blood sacrifice in Wales and that is why she was attacked and had that accident, because with the sacrifice they were trying to kill the holy child in her womb.

Despite everything I always experienced more peace in the house in Belgium. It was so different here than in Wales. Here, life was just normal. But I was stressed also because I never knew when a message would come that I had to go back. Then I had to drop everything, book a ticket and go back that same day.

A loan

In the middle of August my husband and I signed a loan for EUR 4,000. The lady said we had to do this, as there was not enough money for the costs that month. My husband and I would rather we had no loan, but this was an instruction. It would take us three years to pay it off.

My new home

"It's time to come back!" When I read those words on the chat, I started to sigh. No, not yet Lord please! The breaks in Belgium were very short. I just want to spend some time with my husband here. But as usual I dared not to express any of my thoughts. "It is too much work for me and you just need to be here to take care of the children." The lady could feel that the handmaiden was stressed while she gave the lady her daily massage, because the handmaiden was thinking about all the work in the kitchen.

I could sleep in the caravan this time. I was thankful as this was so much better than a tent. This was my private little home on the mountain. But I felt stressed because the lady could watch the caravan from her bedroom.

Every hour

The white Ford Kuga was as good as dead and I had to start it every hour and let it run for a few minutes to keep the engine charged up. The car needed a new battery. I set my alarm on my phone and was hoping it would go off during the nightly hours. This was crazy, another unconventional thing I had to go through. The lady said this was because of my sin, as Michael the archangel told her that I slept more than three hours per night when I was in the little tent. I knew for a fact this was not true. The tent was so small and uncomfortable for me, that I could hardly sleep at all.

Like in the old days

While I was in Belgium again, my husband and the handmaiden had moved the caravan to another place at the side of the house. Here I felt better and less watched and observed. Because the lady was in the white house, I could not go upstairs to use the bathroom, and I did not want to disturb her with my presence either. I just took a big plastic container and used that as my bath tube. I washed my hair outside in a bucket.

Heart-breaking

It was time again to change positions after my little break in Belgium. My husband and I were instructed that we could not communicate with each other, as usual. I arrived in London Victoria Bus station and sought a place to sit down. I found a chair and right before me sat my husband! I saw he was looking on his little device. Everything in me went nuts, here was my husband but I could not speak to him! It was the hardest thing for me to obey this instruction, but I did.

We both arose as it was time to board the busses. My husband was walking right in front of me. He had no idea I was walking right behind him. He stepped onto his bus bound for Belgium and I stepped onto my bus bound for Wales. I was heartbroken to the core, but I never spoke a word to him.

Just using us

"They are just using us! And they wring my husband out like a mop!" I was probably sinning for thinking this, but this went through my mind many times. My husband was always working interim jobs when he was in Belgium. At times he cycled for one hour with his bike to get to his working place. And as soon as he came home, he had to connect online to do the warfare prayers with us all. I knew he did not have the courage to take good care of himself, or eat properly. He just grabbed whatever was at hand. I was hurt and angry because neither the lady nor the handmaiden ever cared how he felt nor did they ever have any gratitude for all the work he did. "They are just using him as a doormat." I heard many times in Wales how they were mocking my husband. Many times we were called "stupid" and "fools".

One day my husband came back from Wales. He looked exhausted, very troubled and super skinny. He could hardly speak. "Is this still normal?" he said while trying to raise his voice. He was taking a bath and tears were running over his face. I looked at him and was shocked to the core. I saw only bones, there was no flesh left on him. He reminded me of those pictures I had seen from those starved people in the holocaust camps. This was beyond terrible. "Haven't they fed you at all?"

Now I was angry at the handmaiden for not feeding my husband. How could she even let him travel this way? And why did you not eat secretly, why are you so obedient and submissive to them like a slave? I knew I had to control my thoughts and emotions quickly, we were told so many times that all this was necessary to kill the flesh, the old persons, and we just had to trust God that He knew what He was doing.

The lady told us the story, when she was doing her 80-day water fast; she looked like a skeleton too, so it was no big deal. I was thinking "It is easier for you, you are part of the two witnesses and you have a special fasting mantle from God." My husband and I always prayed for a fasting mantle, but we were always hungry and fasting was very hard for us. The lady explained this was because we still had so much deliverance to go through.

My husband phoned the lady one day when he was in Belgium. He had to do a 21-day water fast. Since we were always fasting, this was very hard. He was so weak that he fell from the stairs and was on the cold floor for many days. He thought he was dying. Then he managed to stumble to the phone to call the handmaiden. Miraculously she picked up her phone. Then the lady said he could go to the store and just have a little bit of vegetable juice. When I heard that much later, I got angry inside. I did not even know this happened!

Every two hours

I was in Belgium again and one time I went to bed a bit earlier in the evening as I had so much migraine. Once I got up again, I saw a message from the handmaiden on my chat, and I apologized and explained to her why I had not responded to the message she sent me earlier, she told the lady and then rebuked me, and said that from now on every two hours I had to check my email. I was basically already living in the office when I was in Belgium due to the many instructions and also because I did not want to miss any important messages in case there was something urgent to do. Now I had to get up every two hours during the night to check my messages. During the day when I had to go out to do things, I made sure I was back in time within two hours.

Later when I was back in Wales, I told this to the lady and she said "But that was not necessary to do that during the night, only for the daytime." And she just laughed it away.

Only God knew how much migraine I suffered due to lack of sleep in this ministry. Many times I had to stay up the whole night and day to prepare to send out a Last Call message. I had to wait until the handmaiden was ready before I could send the letter out. Many times I could not afford to have some rest just in case I would miss her message that said I had to start sending out the letter immediately. I had to send it all out via a secured email provider, which only allowed me to send out so much per day, so I used different email accounts in groups per fifty. Then I had to send the message to lots of people separately via their contact page on their website, as they did not provide any email address.

Afterwards there was even more work for me to do. I had to put it all on The Last Call website and then check and clean out all the automatic incoming emails, but also emails from angry people who wanted to take me off their list, since they never subscribed in the first place. I had to keep all these names in my files. It was just a lot of extra administrative work and everything took many hours until all was done. The Last Call website was a new website that I had to put together previously instead of the YHWH GLORY one.

Barn under water

On another occasion I received an emergency message that the barn was under water and I had to come to Wales immediately. There had been a thunderstorm and the handmaiden had to move out the big carpet and all the furniture. It was one of those very rare moments that I was with my husband in Belgium.

"Why is there always an emergency when I am here in Belgium?" I cried out. I was not happy when I booked another bus ticket to leave that same evening. I arrived in Wales to expect a drama, however the handmaiden told me that she had taken care of everything already and that the carpet was almost dry.

So I left my husband in Belgium for no urgent reason. Then it crossed my mind they were doing this on purpose to separate us as much as possible. The seasons for me in Wales lasted mostly about three or four months and then I could have a short break in Belgium for about one or two weeks. The breaks came when I began to manifest too much of the "old woman". The lady always knew from God when it was time for me to go back.

One season I could not handle it anymore over there and I

really wanted to see my husband again. I decided to manifest on purpose, so they would send me back. The lady then rebuked me and said that she knew the old woman wanted to go back, and that the old woman did not like it here, but this time I had to get through my deliverance "in the glory" here in Wales so I was not allowed to go back to Belgium.

No time to say goodbye

The message that I did not want to see "It's time to come back!" popped up on the screen. My husband had to come back to Belgium and I had to go back to Wales. He came home at evening time and I had to leave four hours later to catch my bus around midnight. I wanted to spend all my time with him and catch up, as we had not seen each other again for a long time. As soon as he was in the house, I received one message after another with instructions from the handmaiden. It was all computer work and I went through it as fast as I could until I shouted out "Why are they doing this now, they know I want to spend my time with you, we only have a few hours with each other?" "They are doing it on purpose" my husband answered, "so we cannot be together." I was very upset.

The bus started to move and my husband waved goodbye to me. I was on my way again to Wales. I was so extremely sad; a feeling that always got a hold of me whenever I left for Wales. Here are these mountains again. I did not like the sight of these mountains as it was a sign that I was back in Wales for a long season again, with only hard work and rebukes awaiting me.

I did my work diligently, even in my breaks in Belgium. I always had a lot of work to do on the computer for the lady and her handmaiden. This was also the time to do extra work on the website, as this was difficult in Wales, since the internet connection was not very fast over there. I also used my time to organize my files.

No more emotions

One time my husband was rebuked and warned by the lady that he cannot love me more than the handmaiden. There could basically be no more emotions or feelings between us.

Working and cleaning

"How long are you going to be sitting in that chair?" the handmaiden asked me when she came in the kitchen. "Only a few minutes, I had to rest my neck for just a little bit" I responded. I had been busy working in the garden for most of the day. "Well, just make sure you don't sit in that chair too long." I was so tired of her remarks as if she was talking to a little child. I was always working, always busy in the house or in the garden. The property was big, so there was a lot to do. I never sat in any other seat in the house, as it would be defiled by my deliverance. However the handmaiden was allowed to use everything freely and she was going through major deliverance also. I started to wonder about that. Only when I had no internet in the kitchen could I sit in the living room to be able to do my work on the computer.

Last week of October 2018

I was in Belgium and received an emergency call from the handmaiden in Wales. The water tank in the ceiling of her bedroom broke down. The whole floor was flooded with water. She had to work all night trying to dry it up and everything was soaked. I had to go back to Wales immediately.

CONFESSION

October 31, 2018 – Confession

Late at night, I went to the lady's bedroom. I confessed

everything that had happened between me and the Palestinian man. I was convinced that is why the water system broke down, as we had learned that whenever something breaks, there was sin in the house. She said she had no idea, which surprised me but then not really. I reflected back at the time with my mother when I realized that her spirits did not know everything after all. But this was very serious now, so I could not have any wrong thoughts. The lady then said that God told her I only had two more days to confess towards her and the others, and that is why the water system broke down. It was God's Last Call and His mercy on me she said, before things were going to get really bad.

Though later, when a man came to fix the water system, the problem was just a lamp that had to be replaced. This had to be done every year and he said we were very lucky that the whole water tank did not collapse. We had never replaced this lamp since we lived here. The man was annoyed as there was a stack of dead flies in the ceiling where the water tank was. "I am not going to clean this up!" he said. The way he looked at me was enough to let me understand how stupid I had been to not replace this lamp and have all these disgusting dead flies around. I did not even know there was a water tank in this ceiling. This was the first time I ever saw it open.

I had been annoyed with myself as I did not know how things worked in this house. The water system, the pump outside, the regulating of the water flow every day to fill up the pond next door and the heating; all of which was done by the handmaiden. Sometimes she had to go down to the stream on the other side of the field across the street, to fix the blockage in the water pump. Only when they were in Scotland did I find out how to fill up the pond for the fish. The owner had some beautiful koi fish in there, but since we moved in, several had died already. But today, I felt really bad that the lady had to suffer again because of my sin.

When I came down to the kitchen the handmaiden told me that everything that had happened in the last two years was my fault, as it had opened the door to the enemy and the lady had to suffer greatly from it. This included the horrible accident she had this summer with her leg, and all the financial struggles the ministry went through. When I heard that the accident was my fault, I had no more hope left in me to continue on.

November 5, 2018

I was instructed to write a confession letter about all this to another sister who was part of the ministry. She had also travelled to Israel when the lady was there and met the Palestinian. I wrote a very open letter to her, but the letter was much edited by the lady, for example she added this bit: BUT THIS SIN OPENED UP FOR THE DEVIL TO ATTACK A (the Palestinian man), HIS FAMILY AND THE LAST CALL MINISTRY, ESPECIALLY OUR BELOVED SISTER AND HOLY CHILD. BUT MOST IMPORTANTLY, IT PUT ALL OF GOD'S PLANS FOR THE MINISTRY ON A TWO YEAR HIATUS! So I took these parts and added it also in the letter to my husband.

November 6, 2018 – Confession Letter to my husband

This is the part of the letter, skipping the introduction, which I wrote to my husband while I was still in Wales:

"Our marriage has gone through a lot since the very beginning, as I needed so much deliverance and healing from my past. And as you also know, since we are both in the ministry, we have been more apart than together and this has not been easy. Our old souls were fighting with each other more than loving each other through all these seasons. We were rebuked many times for our sin and at a certain times I was instructed not to even think about you anymore or pray for you. I was told we would never see each other again. But then we did. We were both told the Lord had already prepared another man for me. Then at times we had to be together again in intimacy. All this broke something in me John. And it made it even harder for me to love you passionately the few times we were allowed to be together. I had a constant battle and cried out to the Lord so much to know if this was just all the breaking of the old souls in us to make us ready, or if at the end we would indeed not be together anymore. One season I thought yes, then the next season I thought no.

My dearest John, I have been in major sin and we learned already that there are no excuses! I am a married woman, 23 years now, and I longed for and fantasized about another man for more than a year. I felt guilty and hypocritical every day, but at the same time, the thought of being with him made me so happy and excited. It became my route of escape out of the reality of our marriage. I repented to God every day about this. I did longer Esther fasts for me to be able to be delivered from this stronghold that got a hold on me. I prayed in tongues during the day for long periods to be able to be delivered from the old woman, but I did not tell you or anyone else about my sin even though I sensed you knew in your spirit about him. This has affected the ministry and created many open doors for the enemy to come in because of this. Our beloved sister also suffered from this, unknowingly for her at that time that it was because of this particular sin.

About two weeks ago when I was here in Belgium last time, I contacted him via Skype and asked him why he was so quiet. This was an instruction from the handmaiden. I had not heard from him for many months, as he did not want to talk to me anymore. He responded back, but ironically he thought it was our beloved sister who contacted him. He was not friendly at all towards her and he was very angry that he did not get the money he needed and asked for, and said it was her fault that he was now in trouble financially. He did not want to speak to her he said, and he even sent a vomiting emoji face. I then told him this was not the sister but me. I told him our beloved sister prays for every cent that goes out, and that YHWH is in her and that it is HE who decides who gets money. He responded that he could not believe that, and he said he also has the Spirit strong in him. He then asked me to leave him alone. I was very shocked that he would even talk about her this way. I now seriously wondered if this was just all about him getting money, because that thought had come into my mind earlier during the year. At this time I was determined to let him go, as it is clear he now comes against our beloved sister and I do not want to be in the boat with someone who is against her.

Many times I have prayed over the last year to the Lord to give me an open door so I could confess to our beloved sister if this was His Will. I had several chances. Surely any time is the right time to confess and repent? I just did not have the courage to do it and I did not want to talk behind the Palestinian man's back. I was still hoping we could confess together. The Kuga broke down when I came back from Scotland. Our Lord and King Yahushua asked me so nicely through our beloved sister to please make things right with you. I tried to make things right towards you, but could not overcome it, as it felt like the Palestinian man's spirit was so strong and now there was a legal right because I let sin become a stronghold in me. But the Lord made it very clear this week when He called me back to Wales through the breaking of the water system. I knew it was because of my sin.

165

Last Wednesday night (10/31) I finally confessed all this to our beloved sister. But I should never have waited such a long time before confessing. I should have confessed right away. I feel so convicted and realize the seriousness of my sin with the Palestinian, being an adulterer and fornicator for more than a year! I have been a hypocrite towards you John and anyone of this ministry. It feels like betrayal also towards our beloved sister and even to God. I repent of my sin and hope the Lord will still allow me to make things right in my marriage, although I do not deserve a man like you. I realize I have harmed you a lot because of all this. And many times when I blamed you, it was my sin that caused it. I confess to you John that I have not prayed for you as a woman ought to pray for her husband. You already told me you forgive me, but I realize what a horrible woman I really am and I hate myself for it. There is no beauty or anything remotely in me like the woman in Proverbs 31. And there is nothing pure and sweet in me for you to love me.

I feel so bad because our sister was diligently seeking Abba for the reason why everything was at a standstill and his promise to help in America and the Holy Land was at a standstill and even why we were in a bit of a financial bind. He told her that as a ministry everyone had to operate with Holiness and His Righteousness and then in the midst of her injury many things were disclosed to her as he began to reveal much about the iniquity of the people associated with the ministry. Even within the inner circle there was sin in the camp. She kept fasting and crying out to Him. Now it's all been revealed and I feel so very bad like I have failed her and God. THIS SIN OPENED UP FOR THE DEVIL TO ATTACK A (the Palestinian man), HIS FAMILY AND THE MINISTRY, ESPECIALLY OUR BELOVED SISTER AND HOLY CHILD.

Everything that has happened over the last two years in the ministry, when the seed of my sin was being planted, is a consequence of my sin. People came at the gate to curse our beloved sister, the Holy family who had to leave the house and travel around Scotland, the boys going back home, our beloved sister's terrible accident, Judah coming into the group and now the Palestinian being under judgment. Also the "sin" of our brother and sister in the house, happened because of my sin! And the fact our beloved sister, the handmaiden, was judged all the time was because of my sin too, she told me. Not to mention all the other things that happened in between when things were breaking down and sin was revealed.

I honestly do not know how to live with all that, because so many other people are hurt especially our beloved sister and precious Eliyahu. I deserve the death penalty and I don't know what God will do with me now. I have shamed everyone and shown that I cannot be trusted. This is the most horrible revelation/situation ever and I have lost all my hope. I am the complete opposite of the woman that I desire to be: pure, holy, sweet and loving. I have very few words now in my prayers, only I repent and I deserve and accept the consequences. God will decide.

If I love God so much, then why did I come against His 10 commandments every day? I was tested and failed tremendously.

I do pray you may be restored quickly for all the stolen and lost time in our marriage and that you may become the beautiful strong John, because I hindered you so much in this, and that you may be blessed for your faithfulness in our marriage.

I want you to know that despite all this and through all this, I always loved you and appreciate you for many things."

(Editor's note. A few details are taken out of this letter for the privacy of others)

And I added this part in red also to the letter:

"After that month in October 2017, when we could stay in the ministry and house, I thought about the sexual encounters with the others in the group and how God has exceptions for His friends. We received blessings the next year by being in the house to serve there and I also felt God's blessings in Belgium.

I thought God was still considering it, as things change all the time, through the sending of the deer in the woods while I was specifically praying for the Palestinian and me? Then I also believed He would change us both where we could not overcome, when He comes."

Sexual pleasures

The lady told us that we were all God's friends and that the white house we lived in would be used for sex among each other in the end times, when hard things would occur in the world, as a blessing for the Inner Circle. But my sin with the man was no excuse, no matter what I had heard or had been told, and I repented very seriously.

Back in Belgium

That same week I returned to Belgium and confessed and repented to my husband. He said he forgave me, but he also put the guilt on himself, as he said it was his fault that I ran to the Palestinian man. He had not been there for me and not loved me as he should. We forgave each other but I knew I committed the major sin. I also confessed other things I struggled with during our marriage. But so did he, and it was a beautiful time of confessing and forgiving each other. I was so happy we had the opportunity to do this.

November 15, 2018
I wrote two letters, one to the lady and one to the handmaiden and friend:

"Dearest beloved Queen Chara,

The Lord is stirring my heart to write this letter to You to apologize for what I did. Apology is a very weak word in this situation. I do not know exactly how to express myself. I realize what I did with our brother was very sinful and super selfish and I created so many open doors for the enemy to come in and attack You and the ministry.

I am so sorry for everything that happened to You, beloved Queen, and Your household during the last two years because of my sin. I am sorry for all the physical, emotional and spiritual suffering I caused You. I am so sorry that the ministry has been on a standstill for the last two years. I am sorry for all the blessings and breakthroughs that have been held back from You and the ministry during this time.

Waiting on Your beloved King and the birth is supposed to be all about Your happiness & joy. I have robbed You of so many happy moments and I am so sorry for this. I cannot even truly know how this all feels for You. But I do understand that what I did the last two years with our brother was one of the worst things I could possibly do to You. If there is one thing I wish I could undo, it is definitely this. But unfortunately I can't. The harm is done and many people are suffering because of my sinful deeds.

I never intended to hurt You like this. I am so sorry that I ruined so many things in Your life with my selfish foolish actions. While You on the contrary showed all those years Your kindness and beautiful selfless love to me. To hurt You this way is an insult for all You have done for me and I hate the evil inside of me. I am sorry I could not even make You happy or simply bless you when I was around You.

I don't know if I can still be part of Your family, but it is my heart's desire. I don't know if I can still be part of Your friendship, but it is my heart's desire. I want You to know, my beloved Queen, that You are in my heart, no matter what or no matter where I am, and I do love You.

I have to bear the consequences now and I take full responsibility. I am not worthy to ask You for forgiveness, but I do ask & hope for it. And I extend to You and the whole family my sincerest of apologies.

I know just saying 'I am sorry' is absolutely not enough and this letter can never cover up for all the hurt and damage done to You, Your beloved ones and the ministry. I can only pray that You, most beloved Queen of ABBA & Yahushua, will receive a thousand blessings from Heaven instead of all the hurt I have caused You. And that You may celebrate an incredible love very soon with Your beautiful Eliyahu in Your arms."

(Editor's note. The capitals used for You and Your are deliberate)

"Dearest beloved (name of handmaiden and friend),

I want to extend to you both also my sincerest apologies. I am so sorry my beautiful beloved sister for all the judgments that came on your head because of my sin with our brother. That is so very serious and I have no words for that. I am so sorry for everything you had to endure because of this and for all the times your relationship/companionship/friendship with your beloved Queen was attacked & affected because of my sin. I am also sorry for all the extra work you had to clean up the mess when things broke down, because of my sin.

I felt so blessed beloved sister for all the times we could spend together and build up our friendship and relationship with each other but now it feels like I have betrayed you all this time.

I am sorry dearest brother & sister that I gave the enemy an open door to attack you both with sin. I ask you to please forgive me for everything.

May you both be blessed with ABBA's everlasting love and may restoration come quickly to you where I have caused any damage."

December 2, 2018

I received an instruction to write a letter of confession of my sin to the Palestinian man in cooperation with my husband, and edited by the lady.

December 11, 2018

"Do you like it?" I asked my husband. I made a beautiful certificate of marriage vow renewal for my husband on his birthday. I printed it out on a big format and put it in a nice frame. It was still strange for me to put my newest name on any paper, but the lady told me this new spirit was a strong warrior and would help me to get rid of that old woman. Apparently, my other spirit was not strong enough to do that. Kind of disappointing that I needed such a strong spirit to war, but that old woman was really strong in me and simply refused to go out! I warred against my own soul so much and practically tried to destroy her, but until now it had not happened yet. Anyway, I truly hoped things were restored now between my husband

and I. Hopefully, we could see each other more now, or perhaps I would be allowed to move to Wales with him.

I did not like Wales, but we were told that we would be the caretakers of the property once the lady has been taken up to heaven with her children. We would then have to prepare ourselves in the last phase of fasting and prayer to be ready for our taking. But with all the rebukes, my husband and I doubted many times if we would still be part of this all in the end. Maybe only one of us will make it? We started this journey together. My Heavenly Father please let us finish it together! Please do not separate us.

2019 – Medications

Back in Wales I was now allowed to sleep in the barn again and have my room back, since the lady could not return to the barn after her accident, as she was bedridden in her room in the white house. I was happy, not because she suffered so much pain, but now at least she could not walk around and check everything out. Was I evil by thinking this? Because no matter how hard we tried, it was never good enough and we were mostly rebuked for not being in the Spirit. There was just so much more freedom now so I could do my work with a bit more gladness, as I could organize for myself the many tasks in and around the property.

The handmaiden was busy day and night serving the lady, and they trusted me that I would do all the other work. However, I was only allowed to go upstairs to clean the bathrooms and the rooms the children were using. I did it quickly when the lady was sleeping, as I did not want to disturb her with all my deliverance. I did not see her much anymore, just for special occasions, and then I would sit on the floor in the hallway at the entrance of her bedroom.

I had to ask my doctor in Belgium for prescriptions for medication. I felt bad because every time I had to lie to her, as she thought these were for me. These were narcotic medicines for the lady. It would have made me so sick if I even took one. My doctor trusted me and she gave me several boxes at once. The lady told me it was ok to lie for her sake or for her protection. "Just repent and Father will forgive you!" she said. I had to do the same with my general practitioner in Wales. But they only wanted to give me one box at a time.

Back in my room again

I washed the mattress cover that the handmaiden used and put on fresh sheets. Now I wanted to clean the barn and make it all nice again. I could not stand the idea of there being any trace of them left in the barn, it made me depressed. What was wrong with me?

It was night and I heard footsteps coming to my door. Oh no, I will have to get up again to do warfare. Many times I had to get up at night to do extra warfare for the lady, especially when she had birth pains.

"Oh Lord please I repent! Please give me more love in my heart for the lady and handmaiden. I don't have it Lord…. Father please I need help, I don't have anything inside of me that is good, please touch me and fill me up with Your Love for them. Help me to have a better relationship with the handmaiden. I want to love them as myself." With many tears streaming down my face again, this would be one of my morning prayers before I went to the white house. My first task of the day was to open the curtains and clean up the kitchen. I made sure all was nice and scrubbed before the handmaiden came down. I hope she will smell the freshness now in here? I even opened the back door to have some fresh air in the kitchen until the children came down, then the door had to be locked again as they could not go outside.

Meanwhile, I checked for any emails in the ministry accounts. Was there no message from my husband? What are you doing today? Where are you working these days? Are you eating enough? Please stay safe on the road with your bike. How is your mother? All these questions went through my mind. I wiped off the tears from my cheeks. We had been separated so much and so long during all those years. Only a few little moments here and there in between our travels where we saw each other, catching up as quickly as we could, before saying our goodbye's again. Now he had to stay in Belgium most of the time to work full time for the lady, so she could have more money to buy things.

Random rebukes

"You need to go and fight that old woman!" The handmaiden shouted at me. We were in the middle of having a nice conversation in the kitchen and I had just complimented her for the beautiful video she made for The Last Call. I went to the barn but this time I did not repent, as I knew my heart was right with God and I did not manifest anything.

Later the handmaiden told me when I asked her about this, that she was instructed by the lady to rebuke me for the "old woman", but the handmaiden could not find any good opportunity to do it. So she just did it that day without any reason. At another time the handmaiden told me that she had to call me really ugly names and rebuke me hard, but sometimes she could not do this to me, as it was too hard.

Taken over

We were so badly rebuked at times and screamed at, and told

things that did not make sense at all. Then later the handmaiden told us that the lady had been taken over by the evil sea queen for two years. She said this is why she was so mean to us during that time, but we had experienced the same behaviour throughout the whole time.

2019 – Cars

"The Kuga is hardly driving anymore. It has hardly any power left." I went ahead and asked the mechanic and he said the piece under the gear had to be replaced, because the car had so many miles. Eventually the car would lose its power completely. It was dangerous to drive the car this way, because it happened several times when I was on the road. For just a few seconds the car would lose its power and go totally dead. Then I had to recharge the battery. I always kept a powerful battery charger in the car and I drove close to the side of the road to make sure it would not fall apart in the middle of the highway. "That old woman took control again! You were not supposed to ask the mechanic. God will tell the lady when it is time to fix the car. You don't need to do that. The car is fine there is nothing wrong with it. Repent!" It was the handmaiden's job to rebuke me hard again.

"I am not driving that car any longer. It's too dangerous and it hardly moves anymore" I told the handmaiden a few days later. Then the instruction came for me in June 2019 to take the car off insurance and I could use our Ford Fiesta instead. They were not planning to fix the car, as it was too much money. The black Range Rover had been standing there since December 2017 along with a little red Ford KA that was destroyed in June 2020. The lady said we had to give it to a charity organisation but they had to give it up for destruction as the car was worthless. It raised £99. This car was bought for the two Indian boys for when they would have their license, and the lady said that she and her son Eliyahu, the holy child, would drive it too on those small roads in Wales.

Time for skirts

"God says it is time now that you can start dressing yourself as a lady!" All those years I had been wearing these loose wide trousers for only a few Euros. She gave me two long black skirts that the lady had been wearing since 2012. "This one is really anointed. She wore it in Israel to prophesy. And it will be warmer for you, as you can still wear trousers underneath" she said. The handmaiden made the skirts smaller so they would fit me better. They will probably have that same stinky smell, I thought. I remembered these clothes from the time the lady was in our house in Belgium.

Later, I had to bring her big suitcase with her black clothes to Wales. The bus driver in London rebuked me for carrying too much weight. You can only have one suitcase he said. I had two big suitcases, my laptop in a shoulder bag, a big purse and a smaller travel bag. I prayed and eventually he let me take the heavy load without any fine.

I don't want to wear her skirts. Lord, am I ungrateful? Is this really what You want? They are not even nice. This one looks like a bag. Please forgive me for thinking this way. I will wear them and I pray the anointing may help me to get my deliverance. I hope my husband will like them; he always wanted me to wear skirts. Thank you Lord, that I may now become a lady.

Nightly warfare

We always had to do warfare several times per day and night. The handmaiden gave me my dinner, mostly a bit of rice and canned beans, between 9pm and 11pm. When she had no time to warm this up for me then I would go to sleep without food. This happened three days in a row and I was frustrated that I could not even warm up my food myself which took only a few minutes. I got up again at 2.45am to do warfare in the white house. I was rebuked one time for not waking up the handmaiden at that time, because I was not allowed to go upstairs. Also, many times during the night, the lady took a bath while the handmaiden was helping her. I avoided seeing the lady as much as I could, so that she might not suffer from my deliverance.

From that time on, I always went upstairs before 3am to make sure the handmaiden was awake. After warfare I went back to my room in the barn, but mostly I did not sleep anymore.

The chicken
I did groceries and wanted to bless the lady and I paid from our Belgium money for a nice organic chicken for her to eat. The lady said this was the most delicious chicken she had ever eaten as it was bought with love. And because of this, the blessings for me and my husband were set free. So something was about to change for the two of us in a good way. But nothing happened and I wondered how long we had to wait for our blessings.

Rebuked for intimacy
One day we were told on one of the rare occasion when my husband and I were together in Wales, that we could be together in intimacy. The lady encouraged us and was all happy and excited about it. So my husband and I, after a long time of being physically separated, made love with each other. Then afterwards we were rebuked and told that it was a test and my husband needed to have the discernment to know this was a test and to stay away from me. We were also reproached that

we wanted to have sex unnecessarily and so now we had even more demons as we shared them with each other while being intimate. So we now had to bear the consequences.

Phone calls

My husband and I could not have any contact while we were separated. No phone calls, no chats, no emails, unless it was business related the lady said, which meant the finances in Belgium. Only then could I send him a little message. One time I could not stand it any longer and I called my husband. I was hiding in the caravan with my phone. From that time I called him every day in the evening when he was home from work, and we talked for one or two hours. He was always so happy when we talked and so was I.

We also sent messages to each other online and it was just all good and very loving and it gave me so much joy and hope. The handmaiden was running back and forth in the kitchen while we sent messages to each other and I was almost certain that she must have seen it by now, but she never said anything. So I thought it was ok for us to now communicate.

Our 40-day fast was over, although there was no difference in Wales between fasting and breaking the fast, we always fasted. I finished a big task in the garden that had taken me many days. I pruned all the hedges on the side, removed all the weeds and thorns and made it all nice for the King to come. I also worked on the field across the street and did the same thing over there. I made sure the young fruit trees were growing nice and straight, by giving them some extra support sticks, although they were hardly growing and had not borne any fruit since we planted them in 2017. I made everything as nice as possible.

REBUKED FOR TALKING

They found out I had been communicating with my husband over the last month and I was rebuked in the lady's room. She said because of my disobedience, I lost all my rewards from the 40-day fast. "God however had beautiful blessings ready for the two of you, you were about to receive it, but now you lost everything."

I had previously told the handmaiden of all the work I had done in the garden over the last month, and now the lady said, this is why I had to use a pruning knife to trim all those hedges. I thought to myself: I used a pruning knife because there is nothing else available. Good tools were scarce.

Beginning of April 2019 – Back to Belgium

I was having a very hard time and wanted to talk to our lady. I prayed for many days and repeatedly things ran through my mind how I could tell her what was so heavy on my heart. I had to pick up my husband at the bus station because I had to go back to Belgium. We briefly hugged and I talked to him about the situation and things going on that I struggled with. He said we could not talk to each other. "Are you going to obey that now?" I asked him. He agreed with me that we would both pray for an opportunity that night to talk to the lady, before I went back.

It was so stressful and silently we motioned to each other to continue praying. The handmaiden gave us a bowl of rice and beans and we ate it without saying a word to each other. I was so tired of having to treat each other like we were enemies. I had so much love in my heart for him. Why could we not just be loving and kind? It just did not make sense as it did not help us at all.

Finally I was allowed to go upstairs to see the lady. It took all my courage to confront her with the things on my heart. I spoke mainly about the lack of love among each other and hardly any communication or personal interest between us. I explained that I tried to work to have a better relationship with the handmaiden by talking more to her and showing interest in her things and struggles. I also said I did not receive food for a couple of days, while I could eat, because the handmaiden was not in the mood to do it. I also said some other things I noticed from the handmaiden that were not right, also with the children. I expressed my desire to just love each other as one nice family. The lady did not rebuke me but she did not say much either. There was not much time granted to me and I still felt it was not ok that my husband and I were rebuked for communicating over the last month.

It was almost time for me to get ready and leave. With a heavy heart I stepped on the bus and watched the white Kuga driving away. My husband went back to the house and me to Belgium.

April 7 – Rebuke comes

"Beloved D...please sister, Yahushua has been ministering to sister K and is not happy with you. If you have had any wrong thoughts or an unrepentant heart for the ministry and the rebuke she gave you, please repent and ask forgiveness! Yahushua said he does not want you to be on Skype tonight, but please earnestly seek Him about what you need to be specifically repenting of and why you need to ask forgiveness from our beloved sister. We love you."

The one who was in Belgium always connected on Skype to do our nightly warfare prayers together. Though my husband and I had no personal contact during warfare.

"Beloved M,

I repent for feeling unheard when I was with sister that day.
I repent for wrong thoughts towards sister and God about being treated unfairly. I repent for overruling God's instruction to not contact John.

I have been seeking the Lord earnestly about all this the whole time and I truly sense the Lord has ministered to me that I also needed to forgive, that is why I sent you that message on skype Friday. I also sent this picture here below to our sister (at the same time on Friday) to "Violette skype" hoping our sister (and God) would forgive me also for disobeying the instruction to not contact John and for disappointing our sister this way (*as I felt very bad about that*). There was no response from our sister and then that video was sent to me yesterday about "*s (the old woman's name) and link to witchcraft*". I was extremely discouraged when I saw that, and I received it as if the question to please forgive me and the apology for disappointing our sister for my disobedience was not received or granted (which would be fair as God is God)"

On April 8 I wrote this:

"Beloved M,

I have continued to seek the Lord/search my heart and I wanted to clarify something. What I wrote here below the first time from what I repent of, was not meant as an accusation towards our beloved sister or you, I just hope it was not received that way.

What I meant was, that it was not ok for me to feel/think I was unheard (*meaning I wanted some more time to talk with our beloved sister*) at that moment, God is in control of the time and what had to be said, was said. I repent for letting that feeling and thought about being treated unfairly coming in afterwards. With this doubt, pride and rebellion came into my heart and I repent of that also towards our beloved sister, and I repent for still holding on to the thought afterwards, that it was good that I shared things with John and that we prayed and sought the Lord for this, before we mentioned anything to our beloved sister.

It was such a hard battle in my mind, when I was in our sister's room. I started shaking and felt the fear of the Lord in her presence. However, I could not overcome/understand that thought/feeling that it was not ok to contact John for these things. It's pure disobedience towards God and He is right and just at all times, I repent for thinking I knew better than God, and for not surrendering 100% and just embracing our beloved sister's rebuke.

I ask forgiveness from our beloved sister for all these things. I hope and pray I can continue on with everything in the ministry and that the Lord in His Mercy will forgive me and deliver me from these evil spirits of witchcraft, rebellion and pride. My desire is to have a humble, meek, sweet and pure spirit for HIM and nothing of that old any more. I hope I will, with all of us, be worthy and ready to receive the Glory when He comes, and be changed and used for His Glory, that has been my prayer and hope for so many years.

Love *"

Garden
There was a lot of grass to cut in the gardens. When my husband was there, the riding mower broke down again and he

had to go buy a small manual lawn mower. He had been using it while I was in Belgium. He told me it was his sin that the riding mower broke, something was wrong with the brakes.

Now it was my turn, and I did my very best to cut as much as I could. However this took such a long time to just do a little piece. I had to use all my strength to push the mower through the grass.

The farmer arrived on the field to feed his sheep and I stopped. What I was doing was ridiculous and I did not want him to see that. It started to rain a lot and by the time I could cut the grass again, it was so long and I could not get through it anymore. I tried several times and then I gave up.

"I will do it, I love hard work anyway" the handmaiden said. She pushed the little thing in the long grass, but could not move it." She said it was too hard and she ran upstairs to tell the lady. She came back with a smile on her face and said "Oh I have good news! You can call a gardener to come and mow the gardens, because it has to be very beautiful as the King is coming!" I was so happy to hear that, more happy about the gardeners coming than the King coming, because I had heard so many times before that He would come. On those times I had to clean the house and trim the garden like never before, because the King was truly coming.

"You need to repent for calling those gardeners!" "But you told me to call them!" I replied to the handmaiden. Yes, but it was not God's will and you still need to repent. It was probably another test that I failed.

Shabbats
The sun was shining through the little window. I arranged my

bed so I could sit against the wall while looking at the sky and have some sun on my face. The birds were always happy in Wales. I wished I was one of them. They were so free. I always prayed to God when He heard my voice, that it might become as beautiful and as pure as those birds singing their praises. I heard the familiar noise of the farmer's quadbike on the fields on his way to check and feed the sheep. It was still early in the morning everyone was probably asleep now in the white house.

I quickly ran over there to open the curtains, grabbed a bowl of cereal and ran back to the barn. I just wanted to be in my room and not see anyone. I opened my Bible and started reading where I left off.

Later during the day I watched some of the sermons I downloaded during the week. Here in the barn there was no internet. This was the only time I had during the week to relax. Thank You Lord, I am so thankful for my little room, my secret place with You. Here I can be myself and cry out to you from my heart. It is so different here than in the white house. I am hungry Father. I am going to grab some crackers in the white house and a carrot. Is that ok? Father are you hearing me?

It was silent but I felt His presence in this little room. I touched the box that was next to my bed. It was a gift that my husband left for me. A cardboard box covered with some nice wrapping paper with printed flowers. I looked at the list I was writing for him, until he could come the next time. It was just some practical things that had to be done on the property, which I could not do.

Are you thinking about me also my sweet husband? Or are you sleeping longer on the day of Shabbat? I miss you so much. I wished we could be together and take a nice walk in the woods in Belgium. I could not stop crying. Shabbats were especially hard for me emotionally, as loneliness was filling the silence.

Working on Shabbats

"I was rebuked yesterday because I had to spend time to clean up the kitchen, instead of being with Mum." That is how the handmaiden called the lady. The day before was Shabbat so I did not clean the kitchen. From now on, the lady said, I had to clean the kitchen also on Shabbat. "You cannot just sit a whole day in your room." I was angry inside because it was the only time I could spend some quality time reading my Bible and listen to some worship music. I was just spending some time in my secret place.

So every Friday night, after the warfare session, I stayed in the house until early Saturday mornings to clean up the kitchen and make sure all the dishes were put away. I did this as fast as I could, because I still wanted to make the most of it, on my Shabbat with the Lord. This way I still get a full day with Him in my room. Was I getting rebellious in my heart towards the handmaiden and the lady?

Written in my diary

August 6: Complete Entire Absolute Identification with the Lord Jesus Christ

"… for your Father knoweth what things ye have need of, before ye ask him." Matthew 6:8b

The point of praying is not to get answers from God, but to have perfect and complete oneness with Him.

August 14: Discipline

It is very easy to grieve the Spirit of God. We do it by despising the discipline of the Lord, or by becoming discouraged when the Lord rebukes us.

"And ye have forgotten the exhortation which speaketh unto you as unto children, My son, despise not thou the chastening of the Lord, nor faint when thou art rebuked of him" Hebrews 12:5

When the Lord disciplines you, let Him have His way with you. Allow Him to put you into a right-standing relationship before God.

August 26: Daily re-crucifixion

There has to be a daily re-crucifixion of any part of the self-life not already completely dead.

September 21: Prayer

Penetrate with Your Light the dark and secret places of my heart, revealing unrecognized sin, fault or failing. Reveal all within me that is not wholly Yours. Burn out the impurities of my being, the dross of my character refined away, so I can go on strengthened and purified to do Your works.

HE COMES!

Tuesday October 1st: He comes!

My husband came to Wales to celebrate Yom Teruah (Rosh Hashanah). I looked at the nice card I made for him on July 8th for our 24th wedding anniversary. It was looking nice on the little night table. Oh I was so very happy when the time came to pick him up at the bus station. It had been so many months since we had seen each other. We went for a coffee before we came back to the house.

In the evening the handmaiden came in our room and said that we could not sleep together. My husband had to sleep in the living room on the couch, because the old woman was still manifesting in me. She also said that I had to do groceries the next morning. I cried out towards her in anger and frustration. We hoped we could at least share the same bed. We knew we could not be intimate, but not even being allowed in the same room? My husband also reacted angry and frustrated. But we obeyed and he slept in the other room.

Groceries

The next morning, I was on my way to do groceries and I just lost it in the car. I screamed my lungs out to the Lord in anger and despair. I felt completely hopeless because of the separation from my husband all the time and the old woman still being in me. When I came back, I told my husband I was really manifesting in the car.

Thursday October 3

We both got a very encouraging word from the lady especially my husband who got an amazing word. I would be healed and my husband was the lady's prophet. He had been trained over the last years to stand at her side and be her prophet. She said that I would also be at my husband's side and that my testimony would heal others. And that we both had given up everything and this would not be for nothing. Wow, finally some hope again!

That day we both watched the movie of Padre Pio together, as the lady had asked us to do. It touched us deeply. I wanted that love and humbleness that Pio had for his Saviour. The lady had received a new revelation days before that she would go to Greece and live with the friars and that she would be the first woman to be accepted into the community. She said they were the best friends of Yahushua, as they truly consecrate their life fully to God in prayers, consecration and much moderated meals.

We both knew the lady wanted to emphasise, by watching this movie, that this was the lifestyle God wanted for us, sober, fasted and consecrated.

My husband and I embraced each other intensely without words for a while. We knew this was an invitation from the Lord; a question to us: Are we willing to give up everything, including each other for the Lord?

"Yes, we are willing."

We both prayed and expressed our desire to the Lord to live that type of life, sober and completely dedicated, forsaking all and giving Him all to help others to be set free and healed. We asked the handmaiden what she thought of the movie, because she watched it separately and she said it did not speak to her at all. I thought that was very strange.

Saturday October 5: Shabbat
My husband and I spent time together on Shabbat.

Sunday October 6: Service
In the afternoon at 2.50pm we both went to the harvest service in the chapel up on the road. Everyone had the first fruits of their harvest, vegetables, fruit and even milk. I felt a bit ashamed as we did not bring anything. The harvest with us had been very poor and the vegetables did not grow. Also the vine in the greenhouse hardly brought any fruit.

After the service we went to the coffee and tea gathering, and we sat with a very nice and humble family. Their daughter was blind and my husband prayed for her.

During the evening between 9pm and 12pm, my husband disappeared into the lady's room. I was waiting in our room in the barn and thought something was wrong. However when he came back, he was very encouraged. He had received good words.

Back to Belgium

A few hours later I had to bring my husband back to the bus station. It was time for him to go back to Belgium. His bus left at 2:10am. I was determined to become fully the new spirit that I had received both for God and to be a help and a support for my beautiful husband!

Continuing on

For the next few days I continued on in prayer to conquer the evil in me, to purify my soul, not having any desire or control, obedience and accepting His will. I cried out so deeply and intensely and longed to be filled and all saturated with His love. I lay down on my bed and thanked my God for my life and all He did for me. I continued to pray to conquer all my frustrations with the others and believed it were my own sins and imperfections that caused this frustration.

Communion

Many times the handmaiden and the lady were taking Communion together upstairs. However I could never be part of that and that hurt me every time, as it was to show how evil I still was. Was it ever going to change? Was I going to be apart from the lady until she was glorified?

October 20

It was Yahushua's birthday celebration. We all had dinner at evening time in the lady's bedroom. But my heart felt broken as she did not look at nor speak to me. I had some little roses for her that were rejected, and I made a beautiful card for the Lord, which I took back to my room. Then I had to stay in the hallway when they all sang a song for Yahushua.

"Here is your cake, perhaps you are tired and want to eat it in your room?" the handmaiden asked me. There was too much deliverance coming from me. I knew enough, I took the little plate and went to the barn in my room. I was totally heartbroken and cried many tears. When would the deliverance stop?

I wrote in my diary that everything reminded me of the time when I lived with my mother and the neighbours.

Heartbroken ...
So many tears ;;
Everything reminds me of Zelzate.

Too much deliverance WHEN WILL IT
STOP ???

October 22

I regrouped myself and wrote this down in my diary:

"Healing—comforted by my Father—simply allowed to come home—be at ease in His Presence and Security and knowing all is well—Restored completely. This is my desire. He is my hope."

My husband sent me an encouraging word later that day on my computer.

New revelations

The handmaiden told me in the kitchen that the lady is the embodiment of the Holy Spirit and part of the Godhead. I was disappointed. The embodiment of the Holy Spirit indeed! I thought the Holy Spirit was a nice humble part of the Godhead, though very powerful. I did not like it when the lady was manifesting or taken over by Wisdom.

Her face was changing, kind of like my mother's face changed when she was taken over. But this was much worse. And Wisdom was always mean. She explained that the Holy Spirit had never been born on this earth, so this would be the first time through the lady. So she was all in all, even her holy child was Yahweh in the flesh. She also said that the lady suffered with Yahushua on the Cross, that she was part of Him. So in a way she also saved the world. And now a second chance and salvation was coming with the birth of her holy child. I had a hard time about the part of her being the Holy Spirit and her being part of men's salvation. But I did not speak about it.

November 2: Shabbat

I drew a picture of a boat and a bird. The lonely bird represented me waiting as a watchman. I wrote some songs in my diary of Dennis Jernigan which gave me some hope. But my heart literally ached with longing for God's love. There was such a deep pain within me and I just could not stop the flood of tears.

Range Rover

The car had to be fixed and I made arrangements with the garage. It was not driving anymore; it had been standing still since December 2017. It needed a new air compressor and other things. The people from the garage came to the property to look at it, which was about 40 miles of driving. They came on two different occasions. It was a blessing they even wanted to come. The lady wanted to sell the car, but it was worth as good as nothing, and when the men heard I still wanted £7,000 for it, they almost fell over. That was the price the lady told me to ask.

"Why didn't you at least drive the car a little bit around from time to time, you could have avoided many problems. That was not wise of you" the man said to me. They did not know there was a queen upstairs watching and in control of it all. My husband and I had, on several occasions, made comments about the neglected cars, but every time we got rebuked for manifesting old persons. Now I had to wash off the mould in the cars every week. The Range Rover had to be covered for a while, as no one could see this car, the lady said. It was not wise, because that is how it became even mouldier. Also inside the house mould had to be washed off regularly.

As we could not sell the car, it had to come back from the garage to the property. The mechanic told my husband, who was in Wales at that time that the car should not be driven that far, but fixed first completely. The lady told my husband to pick it up anyway. On his way, the car dropped dead. My husband called me while I was in Belgium, to my surprise, and was very frustrated with all these car problems all the time. The handmaiden came and the car started that time, and she drove the car home without any more problems.

Then later, when the invoice came, which was not much, I had to rebuke the mechanic in an email that he charged too much. The man was shocked with my reaction. I was shocked too, because he did not overcharge us at all, on the contrary, and this man had always been very nice to me. One day I even gave him some Belgian chocolates for him and his family.

Relationships broken

It seemed that all relationships were broken in Wales because we had to rebuke the people whom we contacted. One time, I had to bring our car to the mechanic. It was a big Ford garage. We received the invoice and the lady said it was too much money. I had to call them and tell them that I was a minister of God, and they had overcharged me and thus they were judged by God. I called them, but did it much milder than the lady told me to do it. The lady made it seem that everybody was overcharging us, which was absolutely not the case. Therefore it was very stressful for me to make appointments with people.

One carpenter did not want to come anymore, he always had an excuse why he could not come and I did not blame him, because I probably would have done the same.

We were using a lot of electricity and the bill was huge every month. I had to make so many calls to the electricity company and spent hours figuring out what went wrong. The lady judged the company and I had to look for another supplier. The new supplier charged us the same amount and asked me what I was doing in the house, since no household spent so much every month, except the businesses.

The lady and handmaiden left all the lights on day and night. Also many times the oven in the kitchen was left on for hours without any food in it. Extra small heaters were on the whole night in empty rooms eating up electricity. We had several freezers. My husband and I tried to make this all clear to them, but to no avail.

Emails

Many emails were also written by the lady in our name, which I did not like. I understood she had to stay hidden for the baby's sake, but many times they were lying to people and making up stories. I did not understand how this was all ok, as God was Holy. But we were also taught that there were exceptions for the lady, these things were part of the mysteries in heaven.

November 17: Get ready

Day 77 of a 100-day fast—5 am: We were going to have a computer call with the lady. She was talking about seal six happening now—the red horse in the book of Revelation. We had to ask ourselves if we were ready as the army of Yahushua and we were told to stay in the fear of the Lord. We had to keep warring and the Lord spoke through her that He needed willing yielded vessels. The revival would start with the two witnesses. We and the heavenly host were all ready and she reminded us to stay faithful till the end.

The lady explained that we started eight years ago in 2011 with the preparation, warning time, consummation, wilderness time, repentance, fasting and prayer time. "You will all be here when the baby is born." She was referring to our rental house in Wales. Wow this was such an encouragement, it truly sounded like it was very close now. "You will be changed, transformed, transfigured and do great things. Don't be cut off guard, be wise." She said it was very important now to get things out of us and get things in from heaven during this time of fasting.

She repeated again that we would all come when the baby was born. Our little group was the team for the two witness ministry. "You all have been found worthy." That was all we needed to hear! The lady encouraged us to spend time with Yahushua "in the garden" and that we would start to ascend. She called it the spiritual and soulish raptures.

Later I tried to picture my secret place in heaven and was ready to make a drawing of it in my diary, however those pages were left blank.

December 8

I longed to be filled with the Love of Yahushua, I have such a pain in my heart for His love. "A supernatural transformation today. His Love is my only desire for my 100-day fast. May it be heard in Heaven today." That was my prayer in my diary.

Back in Belgium

I was with my husband in Belgium on his birthday December 11. We were wondering if we could even celebrate it. We decided that we would go out and eat something together. We had a vegan lasagne and one glass of wine together. This had not happened in many years. We enjoyed it and had a very good time together.

Christmas was coming and the lady had said we could celebrate it together. This was a dream come true! However my husband had to go back to Wales before Christmas time, which was very disappointing. He wrote this in my diary:

And without faith it is impossible to please God, because anyone who comes to him must believe that he exists and that he rewards those who earnestly seek him.

Hebrews 11:6

December 15 afternoon

-♡- Darling -♡-
Will you run this race with me... ??
Close bey my side,
One from a distance
        United in Him,
        A tree-fold cord can not be broken easely.

You will always be in my heart
Run into His Arms,
Your first LOVE.
And everything will be allright.

        Keep Running...
        This your New Demension
Step up your horse
And run, run into eternety
He will meet you there.

MARINE SPIRITS

Marine spirits

The lady had told me many times that I was affected by marine spirits and that they had stolen my soul and parted it into pieces. She also told me the most horrific thing someone can ever hear: She said that as a baby, I was sacrificed by my mother as the bride of satan. When I heard that, I was totally upset. I loved God so much, how could this have happened? I had no memories whatsoever. I always detested horror movies and anything to do with devilish things. Yes, my mother was involved in the occult and paranormal things, but she would never do such a thing? She was just very much deceived. The lady told me also that she was a high priest.

Before she told me all this, I had asked the lady if my mother was in Heaven. She said yes, that she was saved, but had no house. Oh well, at least she is in Heaven and she will be happy I was thinking. I had to send testimonies to the family and I also sent one to the neighbours from the past.

Afterwards the lady told me that my mother was not in Heaven, but in one of the worst places in hell, and then she told me these horrific revelations.

Retrieving back my soul

So I did lots of warfare prayers against these marine spirits and believed at a certain time that I had retrieved back my soul.

Christmas 2019

My mother-in-law was in the house with me and I made a nice meal for us. Chicken for her but not for me. I stayed vegan. My husband was in Wales. We were never together on these days.
I travelled back to Wales the last week of December after

Christmas. My husband and I did strong warfare against that "old woman" and he prayed three hours for me. I truly believed she was manifesting as I heard a voice in my head pleading for mercy.

December 30

We never gave gifts to each other on birthdays. The lady said these were the old souls, and we could not celebrate those. However now I received a gift from the lady on my birthday. It was a thick book called "The Jehu Prayers" from Dr Olukoya. It was a book loaded with prayers for deliverance.

"Could they not give you something else for your birthday?" my husband said. "I know...." I replied. But I was happy to have this book as I wanted it anyway. I started using it immediately.

Talking at the gate

My husband and I went outside in the garden. Immediately we talked about the doubts we had and strange things going on. "That is not normal anymore, I feel afraid when I am here alone, I just feel.....it's like a demonic presence...." I said to my husband. He kind of agreed with me, and we were standing at the gate of the barn where no one could see or hear us. "I have so many thoughts about just running away....." These thoughts had come to my mind many times over the last year. I had planned every possible escape route in my head. I just wanted to run away and never come back to this place anymore. I had doubts about the lady's holiness and many things just did not make sense. Also the constant separation and the consecration, it was all so mysterious but we all just continued on day by day, year after year. It was now 6 ½ years that the lady had been pregnant and there was still no baby born. Would it take seven years?

Friday January 3, 2020

The handmaiden told me I had to go back to Belgium and that no one could be there anymore as the glory became too strong. And now the holy child would be born. But my husband had to stay in Wales. Little did I know this would be the very last time that I would ever see this place? I was back in Belgium on Friday January 3.

Tuesday January 7, 2020

I took a bath and when standing up I became very dizzy. It turned black before my eyes and I went unconscious and woke up with a loud noise in my ears and blood dripping from my chin. I held the metal rod in my right hand that was broken off the wall, what happened? Was I just weak because I was Esther fasting for two days? I was scared and felt a demonic presence, then I knew this was an attack from the enemy, I could just feel it. Was he trying to kill me?

I looked in the mirror and saw a big gap in my chin. I could stick my finger in it. Oh this didn't look good. It still felt sedated, but I was extremely dizzy and could hardly move. I called my husband. He told the lady and she said it was God's way of delivering me, but it was no sin. She told me to put honey on the wound. I looked this up online and it was indeed a very good method to heal open wounds quickly. I disinfected the wound first, then put organic honey on it, and covered the wound with a compress. The next day I took off the compress and the wound was completely closed. Wow, this was a miracle.

I now understood that I had fallen and banged my chin on the edge of the marble sink while I went unconscious.

Saturday January 11: Heal and detox

While I was reading my Bible I received in my spirit that this was a season to heal and detox from people, from old habits and from wrong spirits.

Saturday February 1 – Back from Wales

In the evening my husband returned from Wales. He just had to sign some papers concerning my health insurance. I was instructed to book a ticket so he could go back the next day. I prayed to God that there would not be a bus available, as I wanted to see my husband for more than just a few hours.

He wanted to go with me for a walk in the woods, as he knew I liked that place so much. He also restored the shower that was broken off and bought a new rain shower. He quickly installed it before he left. It was a gift that he bought for me and I was so happy with this blessing.

He was also worried about the dizziness I had, I still had to hold onto the furniture at times so that I would not fall.

CHAPTER VI: OUR LAST GOODBYE

TUESDAY FEBRUARY 4 – BACK TO WALES

The first bus available was Tuesday morning. My husband was loading his suitcase onto the bus. I did not like this bus anymore. It broke my heart every time I saw it. It was super hard for me to let him go again. I watched his every move and he waved at me when he found his place in the bus. I hoped the bus would never leave. But it did and with tears in my eyes I waved goodbye to him, one more time. I watched the bus until it disappeared into the traffic. I was walking the streets heartbroken to find my local bus back to our house. I opened the front door of the house and when I went in, that loneliness greeted me and got a hold on me once again, that feeling that had tormented me for many years.

I had no idea I would not see my husband again for a very long time. I loved him so much we just did not have a chance to show it to each other.

Dizziness

The dizziness was not really getting better and I went to see the doctor. She said I had a concussion, but that it would heal. I went to a physiotherapist to massage my neck and after a few times she did a special manoeuvre, something came out of the tube of my ear with that hard fall in January, which was now flowing around in my ear, and it had to be brought back into the tube. With a special but drastic manoeuvre we hoped that this would fix the dizziness. It worked as the dizziness got less intense and eventually disappeared.

March 2 – 7 day Esther fast

On March 2nd my husband and I started a 7-day Esther fast, no food nor water, which we completed successfully. The lady said it was for the salvation of the Jewish people.

Since my husband left, we called each other almost every day. We did not know if we were allowed, but we did it anyway. It was so good every time and we lifted each other up. My husband always told me how encouraged he was after every phone call. He always called me when he was on his way to the chapel on the road to pray. The lady told him he needed to go there every day to pray and seek words from Father for her. It was stressful for him to be forced every day to receive a word or a vision.

March 12, 2020 – To the U.S.
My husband was instructed to go the U.S. to bring a lady to Wales. This was the young lady who tried to come before, but was sent back because she had no return ticket. The lady said then that she had too much deliverance and she was not ready. Now she was ready to come. Her eyesight was not good, so my husband was there to help her. He called me as there were some problems with the tickets and if I could help him out.

It was the time during our weekly Esther fast and on their way back my husband called me and wondered if it would be ok for him to eat something as he was so weak. I advised him that I thought it was ok. Later he was rebuked by the lady because he had eaten something small. The young lady and my husband arrived in Wales on Monday March 16.

Not going back again
On one of our last phone calls my husband told me I would not come to Wales anymore. He was making it clear not to get my hopes up on that, because I still needed too much deliverance. The lady told him I was married to him so I could be saved. He

was also trained to be a prophet to stand at her side, and I could not stand in the way. That reminded me of the time when I could not stand in the way between my mother and the neighbour woman when we were separated. Was I really that evil? But he also said that the lady had a vision about me and my husband's castle in heaven. Ok, now I was a bit more encouraged. He also said it would be close to the lady's palace so now I felt discouraged again. What was wrong with me?

The dragon

During the last years I was reminded regularly about a dream the lady had about me that I was part of the dragon out of Revelation 12. That revelation was another thing that made me feel I was still so much more evil than anyone else in her inner circle. So it was too dangerous for me to be around the holy child, as I could hurt him. I knew in my heart I would never do that, and despite the resistance deep inside of me that I felt all those years but could not really explain, I always served the lady with all that I had in me, with all my strength, heart and even our money. My husband and I had given it all. Every month, I even rounded up the amount for our monthly tithe and many times I gave something extra for the lady and trusted God for my needs in Belgium.

Other people coming

On March 14 one of the two boys that went back to London was contacted by the lady and he was on the train on his way to wales. She told him that he had to come back right away. He was now 19 years old so he could do whatever he wanted.

Another lady was also invited to come and live in the house with the lady. She had been a good financial supporter for many years. Now I really felt bad, as the handmaiden told me when I left the house on January 3rd, no one could be in the house anymore, yet three new people had come by now. When would it be my turn? Or was it really true that I would never go back again like my husband told me?

Computer

One day the handmaiden needed a new computer to make the videos for "The Last Call". My husband contacted me and said he really thought we should tell them that we had cash in the house. This was the only cash and extra we still had, we kept it separated, because I had to pay this amount back to the insurance office, since they overpaid me. I knew, when I told the handmaiden, that I would have to give the money back straight away. I gave it to her with all my heart anyway and she used it to buy her new computer. The lady said that my husband and I would have a baby soon now, because I had given the money right away. This filled my heart with new hope and joy.

A miracle happened because I never had to pay back this money to the insurance. I even called them many months later to make sure and they said I did not had to pay back anything and all was ok.

Caught

My husband called me and said we could not communicate anymore with each other. We were chatting online and I was really pouring out my heart to him, I was very discouraged that day about us being so separated etc. It looked like I was manifesting the "old woman" big time. My husband was sitting in the caravan to hide from the others, and at that moment the handmaiden came into the caravan looking for him. She saw we were chatting, she told the lady and that was the end of our calls and chats.

END OF CONTACT

Fasting and repenting

I continued to fast as much as I could, Esther and water fast. In between I stayed on a vegan diet. I really wanted to get my deliverance from that "old woman" and did my best to stay very positive and let go of my husband. I did a lot of serious warfare for myself, to break off all curses and demonic influences. I was very repentant and even put ashes on my head at times to humble myself before God.

March 31, 2020

I wrote a letter to the lady, for something wrong that I had done. The handmaiden's computer passport was ruined and all her videos from The Last Call were gone. It was my job to download the videos again on the YouTube channels, as I had them all saved on my computer. However, at that time it did not occur to me that I had to set the video first to high quality, so most of the videos were now downloaded in poor quality. But I repented for that and told the lady I was very sorry.

April 19, 2020

I had prepared a special gift for the lady's 50th birthday. I had sought a company who could embroider a text in different colours and fonts on a hooded baby towel. I found a small company that was not too expensive, and had loving words from the lady and her King, that I took from a prophetic song from the lady, embroidered on the baby towel with a crown on top of it. It was really beautiful and very unique. I added a nice card and I could not wait to send it off and wait for the lady's reaction. She was very pleased and happy with this unique gift.

Warfare files

I had been given the instruction to put together a file with all the warfare prayers that we daily used and other prayers as I was led. First I had to edit them all, which took a lot of work and I added nice pictures on the background. I looked for any prayer that could be useful. Then I printed them off and put all the pages in high quality plastic sheets. I added numbered and coloured tabs and ordered the sheets into the right category. These all went into a file folder and I made a List of Contents.

I made a file for the household in Wales and a separate one for the lady which I decorated with hearts. It was another big box that was sent to Wales.

May 17, 2020 – Baby announcement

ELIYAHU YERMIYAHU YESHAYAHU YAHUSHUA Who is ordained to be Birthed in this Exact Time. As she has been carrying Yahushua's Holy Child miraculously for nearly 7 years now, since July 22, 2013 … Suffice it to say: IT IS TIME!"

Another baby announcement was sent out with an invitation to bless the holy child. A list was put together and I had to make a nice presentation of it all.

July 8th – Wedding anniversary

Today my husband and I have been married for 25 years. Wow, I could not believe it had been that long. What happened to all those years? I was sad as we did not really have a wonderful past to look back on. Another anniversary without my husband that went by and no one even cared. We were still not allowed by the lady to contact each other.

Later I found out that the lady sent an email to the landlord in my and my husband's name, telling him how we were celebrating our anniversary together even wich champagne. It broke my heart even more when I read this. These lies started to make me angry and upset.

Last fish dies

"Have you been sinning? Have you been in contact with your husband?" the handmaiden asked me over the phone. "No I have not" I answered frustrated. "Good, I thought you wouldn't, but the last koi fish died and there is sin in the camp".

July 22nd 2020

The seventh birthday for the holy child was coming up and I had prayed and prepared a big box with nice gifts. I was always looking for nice gifts for the lady, even when I was in Wales which I paid with our Belgium money. Now I had three coffee mugs printed with prophetic pictures that I made and matching scriptures. I also had a selection of the finest chocolates and biscuits and organic cheese that I knew the lady liked. And some other small gifts to decorate her room. Everything was packed carefully in bubble plastic. I put a label on top of the box stating that this could only be opened by the lady, as I wanted her to unpack it. Of course, she was very pleased and happy again with these special gifts.

September 17, 2020

Rosh Hashanah was here and I wrote a personal letter to everyone in the house in Wales, this is a short excerpt from my letter to the lady:

"The pain and regret I feel from all my sins is a very heavy cross to bear. I have begged the LORD with many tears to pierce my heart with His weapon, and let it bleed pronouncedly, so it could be purged and re- created into something beautiful, so I could never hurt any single soul again, but instead to love them, like HE did. That for me would be the greatest Gift ever and is all I long for."

Thanksgiving

After thanksgiving I received a picture on the chat with everyone that was in the house. I saw my husband sitting at the corner of the table. They were all dressed in white and the lady was dressed as a queen. I stared at my husband and tried to figure out if he was looking well or not? He looked different!

End November – Breaking of the long fast – Urgency in me

After we all broke a 100-day fast end November 2020, I suddenly got this "emergency" in me that my husband had to come back to Belgium. My husband had been in Wales since January 2020, but it was such a convincing feeling inside of me by the Spirit that I could not shake it off. I even rebuked my own flesh for wanting him to come back, as I was already told by the lady we would never be together until we were glorified.

I sought the Lord in prayer and tears for what He was trying to tell me, crying out for three days.

December 5, 2020

I sent these messages to the handmaiden:

"I wanted to ask you something, can John come to Belgium during the Christmas time? Now that we are all off the most intense fasting, would it be allowed? It's been almost 1 year that we have not seen each other and I really miss him. It would be so encouraging if we could have some time together now. John could travel easily back and forth. He just has to fill in a form and put on paper that he will stay here in the house for quarantine for 14 days. I just miss my husband a lot, and it would be a huge blessing if we can spend some quality time together and with the Lord."

The handmaiden replied:

"Beloved you know this would not be wise at all; and not safe for our beloved Mum and baby if John went to Belgium. Would H really ask this question, or do you need to fight that old woman? This is a critical time right now to FOCUS ON THE JOB AT HAND and we all must BE READY at all times for Yahushua's Coming! We love you sister; keep going with your deliverance and purification! He is assessing everything right now, and He is coming quickly!

Dearest H, in all tests and in everything we don't understand about ABBA's Ways, He looks at our HEARTS. I pray we will all stay faithful & true to Yahushua, His Bride & Holy Child (the Two Witnesses of Rev 11&12) in wholehearted obedience to Father's Will. For I have seen personally sister, the LORD has made her rich and He certainly will add no sorrow with it. Look at the Blessings He has bestowed upon her since 5781! If there was sin, would she be living in such a heavenly blessing? I know we know the answer to this deep in our hearts. Her Knight in shining armour is about to sweep her up and take her far away from all of us. And I've cried many tears, sister, because of the loss this earth will experience with the taking of His Beloved Queen and Holy Child. WOE unto all of us with unclean hearts and unclean hands, and mouths that speak guile before the Most High YHWH ELOHIM, for She is One of Them! Again I say to you: WOE unto us. May YHWH have Mercy!"

December 11, 2020

It was my husband's birthday and I asked the lady if I could make a nice card for him. She said yes and I sent it to the handmaiden's email. She said she had printed it out for him and that they gave my husband a nice new cover. I was hoping they would give him a nice dinner too. I felt frustrated and sad because I had to ask permission to send a birthday card to my husband that had to be reviewed first by the lady and I could not even give him a gift nor talk to him.

My beautiful beloved John,

Today is your special day and I wish you a very Blessed Birthday & I pray God's Special Presence and Love may be with you, that His Goodness, Mercy, Love & Grace may saturate you and everything that you need, every day ♡. I think about you every day, every night and I miss you so much. I love you dearly and long to be in your loving embrace. A big Hug and many sweet kisses for you from me ♡ ♡ ♡

Love you lots Hannah xxxx

But as for me and my house, we will serve the LORD.

HUGE REVELATION

December 14, 2020 – Huge revelation

I sought the Lord in prayer again, crying out for many days to Him for the truth and an answer. Then in the woods, after a long walk while praying and crying, I finally heard a still small voice that said: "There is deception" and that it is the time for things to be exposed now, and that we would help many others by testifying of the things we witnessed, as many are under this type of deception.

I answered: "For sure You do not mean K~ (the lady) Your Bride, Your Wife?"
He said "Yes!".

I heard this Scripture: *"Notwithstanding, I have a few things against thee, because thou sufferest that woman Jezebel, which calleth herself a prophetess."*

He also said: "I gave her time to repent." I was so terrified of the Lord that I did not even want to hear it anymore and stopped listening.

But I still heard: "At the mouth of two witnesses, or at the mouth of three witnesses, shall a matter be established. I shall give you three witnesses." I said frustrated and fearful at the same time "Well, then give me three witnesses!"

When I came home, I looked up the Scripture in Revelation 2 and it further said: 22 *"Behold, I will cast her into a bed, and them that commit adultery with her into great tribulation, except they repent of their deeds."*

Within 24 hours I got three witnesses of people who received the same scripture and they all knew it was talking about the lady. And I did not share anything beforehand about all this. This is how we in our little prayer group started to talk about the revelations God was showing us now, and we even fasted and prayed and asked others that we did not even knew personally to do the same. They all confirmed to us in ways hard to deny this was God trying to tell us something. We continued to pray and ask for confirmation and we received daily confirmation. A key scripture that we all kept receiving was that "He would open the Red Sea".

Revelation 2:20-21

"Notwithstanding I have a few things against thee, because thou sufferest that woman Jezebel, which calleth herself a prophetess, to teach and to seduce my servants to commit fornication, and to eat things sacrificed unto idols. 21 And I gave her space to repent of her fornication; and she repented not."

December 16 – Jezebel

My online friend shared her daily devotional with us, and the scripture reference on the devotional was Revelation 2, the Jezebel Scripture. This was not planned!

December 17, 2020

A sister sent a video to my friend and she did not know at that time about all these details going on in our lives. The title of the video was: "Signs of Jezebel influence".

December 18, 2020

Me: "Beloved (name of handmaiden), Will you please send this to Mum (the lady's name).

I really desire to spend Christmas time with John here. Just a few days we can have together to enjoy and do some simple things, like a walk in the park, a bike ride or have a nice meal together, and then he can visit Oma (his mother) also. They make it easier now to travel these days.

We did not communicate with each other at all for a full year now almost. I do love John very much but I am overwhelmed with grief and I just want to see him and give him a nice big hug.

Everyone in the street keeps asking me about John and they remind me he's been missing for a year now. They know the borders are open. They don't understand that he does not even come to visit his mother. I just start crying all the time. If he could come for a couple of days, so people can see him, and see us together, Oma can see him, I sense that would be a good thing for everyone. And it is also Oma's birthday this month and she has been very sad that she has not seen John for so long, she misses him too. And it would encourage me very much too."

December 20, 2020

Me: "Beloved (name of handmaiden),

I sent you two messages before that I really want to see John and spend Christmas time with him. I told you I am very sad and so is Oma, after being apart for a full year, and we simply want to see John and have a few days with him. That is all I am asking.

I have booked two tickets for him to come. The National Express bus leaves SWANSEA TUESDAY DEC 22 at 08:15 am His next bus leaves LONDON at 20:00 pm National Express Service: NX 507 Date of travel Departure Tue Dec 22 08:15 SWANSEA Bus Station"

Me: "(Name of handmaiden) why are you ignoring my other messages? I have been separated for a full year from my husband, and I am at the end of my tether. I want to speak with my husband over Wire right away. I have a right to simply say hi and talk to him.

Belgians are allowed to travel abroad. I can't agree anymore with the fact that I cannot even talk to him. That is not ok and not even biblical. Everyone would agree with me on that. I am asking you one last time, please connect me with John over Wire right now. If you don't allow us to, I will stop all ministry work, finances and everything until we connect."

The handmaiden: "Mum will address this with you once she gets back from the courts of Heaven. Be careful you are on thin ice and she was summoned just now to YHWH.

ALL TRAVEL HAS BEEN STOPPED IN WALES. SORRY SIS."

Me: "That is not true only the airplanes and the trains, the buses still drive and Belgians can travel."

The lady: "YOU DEAR NEED TO REPENT. THE EVIL SEA QUEEN IS AFTER YOU! BESIDES, ABBA HAS TOLD US NOT TO TRAVEL HERE UNTIL HEARING OTHERWISE FROM HEAVEN. YOU ARE GROSSLY OUT OF THE WILL OF THE LORD."

December 23, 2020

Me: "You know beloved sister, I am going through a very intense emotional time, and I just need to spend more time in prayer and more time with the Lord. I am not up right now to do any website or ministry work, I cannot even focus on that right now. I hope you understand."

The handmaiden: "Beloved H, Mum received that Abba is giving you one week to spend extra time in prayer and get yourself back together to resume all your responsibilities for His Ministry. You have a very important position H, and He

214

has entrusted you with much! Thus, much is required. So don't give up! Keep going and choose to be an Overcomer IN HIM! Do you sense you should start on a water fast soon?"

December 28, 2020

The handmaiden: "Will you please send the Belgian medication for beloved Mum? Thanks sis ❤"

December 29, 2020

The handmaiden: "Do you have an appointment with your doctor any time soon? The medication from Belgium is more effective for her than the brand from Wales, and it really helps her get through all intense pains as she daily carries her cross with Yahushua until He comes.

Please H, help us in this thing that only you can do for our beloved Mum, as YHWH has appointed you to provide a way for her to manage the pain. 👣☺"

December 30, 2020

The handmaiden: "Sister, you would rather our beloved Mother suffer in major pain when Abba YHWH has provided this way for her to endure? You KNOW she can't go to a doctor, so He has chosen you to go in her stead! The truth is you ARE in pain. And the truth is, you need this medicine because it is God's Perfect Will that you receive this medicine for her! The Holy Child must be protected, and this is why you have helped to keep Him safe all these years by standing in her place for purchases and even this place that was prepared for her to stay and keep her hidden! Do you even care about keeping her safe anymore sis?"

A CULT!

By now we all had the revelation that we had been trapped in a CULT "THE LAST CALL OF YHWH ENDTIME MINISTRY" also called "YHWH יהוה IN THE UK ENDTIME MINISTRY".

All these doubts, resistance in my heart, the continuous unrest and fear, all the separation and broken relationships, were not "the old woman" manifesting. It was the still small voice of the Holy Spirit warning me!

For 8 ½ years I had tried to destroy my own soul by doing very strong warfare against her, I fasted seriously all the time and slept very few hours. I had given my whole life to God, my house, my country, my food, my comfort in all my physical pains. I worked hard day and night, I gave up my husband for all those years, I broke every relationship in my life, I cried out to God every day in tears to kill my flesh, seeking His leading and guidance. Yes I was still deceived.

I have come to this Conclusion and Reality in my life: TRUE REPENTANCE INCLUDING <u>TURNING AROUND AND CONFESSING TO OTHERS</u> WAS A NECCESITY AND THE KEY TO MY FREEDOM.

After eleven months of physical separation from the lady, I started to hear that still small voice of the Holy Spirit that convinced me to the core of my being, even without words at first, that something was very wrong in Wales and that my sweet husband was in danger. I cried out to God in all seriousness for several days. I did not hear anything, no voices, it was pure silence. I thought that God had forsaken me.

Then one day, while I was praying in the woods, the Holy Spirit made it very clear to me, with very few words, what was going on. He gave me a Scripture and He gave me three witnesses within 24 hours.

I started to repent immediately, I confessed to my husband's family, to my family, to the church and to others who had been hurt or deceived. They forgave me.

John 8: "When Jesus had lifted up himself, and saw none but the woman, he said unto her, **Woman, where are those thine accusers? hath no man condemned thee?**

11 She said, No man, Lord. And Jesus said unto her, **Neither do I condemn thee: go, and sin no more.**

12 Then spake Jesus again unto them, saying, I am the light of the world: he that followeth me shall not walk in darkness, but shall have the light of life."

January 3, 2021
The phone rang. It was my husband. Last time I heard him was in March 2020. I could hear he was extremely nervous, not himself at all, and I heard someone whispering next to him. He refused to speak in Dutch, so I talked in Dutch and he in English.

He did his best to raise his voice when he said:
"You have never been submissive and always been in control. I am your husband, now you need to listen to me, because you never listened to me in the past. I demand you to send your money and my mother's money. I demand you to put the website online again. I demand you to buy the medications for k~ (the lady), as she is in tremendous pain with her leg. He said I harmed him and everyone else over there by sending the police. Do you know that Father is divorcing us now in heaven?

217

Did you know that? Judgement is coming your way."

This was not my husband. He never spoke to me this way in all those years. It was very clear he was instructed what to say. I tried to talk to him in between loving and calm, but he hardly listened. He just overruled me most of the time. I knew for a fact this was all foretold to him by the lady. Then I heard the handmaiden, with a sweet soft voice she said to me. "Hi, it is ok if you don't want to be part of the ministry anymore. But if you…." Then I put the phone down. There was no way I was going to talk with her.

I was extremely grieved that my husband was so brainwashed by the lady, and that he was in so much fear. The things he told me over the phone were pure manipulations from her part, to get money and medication. It was clear that he did not even speak with his sound mind anymore. And they probably forced him into extreme fasting. Lack of food is a big way to control people as this has a huge impact on your emotions.

I planned to send him a postcard nearly every day with just some simple love notes, so he would know I loved him dearly. Hopefully his heart would melt again?

Zechariah 4:6: *"Then he answered and spake unto me, saying, This is the word of the LORD unto Zerubbabel, saying, Not **by** might, nor **by** power, but **by my spirit**, saith the LORD of hosts."*

Acts 9
3" And as he journeyed, he came near Damascus: and suddenly there shined round about him a light from heaven:

*4 And he fell to the earth, and heard a voice saying unto him, **Saul,***

Saul, why persecutest thou me?

5 And he said, Who art thou, Lord? **And the Lord said, I am Jesus whom thou persecutest: it is hard for thee to kick against the pricks.**

6 And he trembling and astonished said, **Lord, what wilt thou have me to do?** *And the Lord said unto him, Arise, and go into the city, and it shall be told thee what thou must do."*

Hope Grace and Mercy

In the following months I had the desire to dive into the Word of God and just "come home" again. I bought a brand new Bible and started to read it like a child, as if reading it for the first time and not seeing it through the lens of the deceptive and twisted doctrines of the cult. The deception had been long and very deep and so it is a hard process to unravel the lies in my head and to establish the Biblical principles and truth again in my life. Examining Biblical passages is so enlightening and it is necessary to put things in the right perspective.

I am very edified and reconfirmed through the teachings of Derek Prince. Derek Prince asked God one day: *Would You tell me what is witchcraft?*

He believes this is the answer God gave him:

"Witchcraft is the attempt to control people and make them do what you want by the use of any spirit which is not the Holy Spirit. If any person has a spirit which he or she uses, it is not the Holy Spirit, because the Holy Spirit is God and no one uses God."

Galatians 5: 19-21

19 Now the works of the flesh are manifest, which are these; Adultery, fornication, uncleanness, lasciviousness,

20 *Idolatry, **witchcraft**, hatred, variance, emulations, wrath, strife, seditions, heresies,*

21 *Envyings, murders, drunkenness, revellings, and such like: of the which I tell you before, as I have also told you in time past, that they which do such things shall not inherit the kingdom of God.*

Hebrews 10:14

For by one offering he hath perfected for ever them that are sanctified.

A very important aspect for my healing is learning to find the divine mercy and freedom of Jesus Christ again and knowing that God is loving and forgiving.

1 John 1:5-10

5 *This then is the message which we have heard of him, and declare unto you, that God is light, and in him is no darkness at all.*

6 *If we say that we have fellowship with him, and walk in darkness, we lie, and do not the truth:*

7 *But if we walk in the light, as he is in the light, we have fellowship one with another, and the blood of Jesus Christ his Son cleanseth us from all sin.*

8 *If we say that we have no sin, we deceive ourselves, and the truth is not in us.*

9 *If we confess our sins, he is faithful and just to forgive us our sins, and to cleanse us from all unrighteousness.*

10 *If we say that we have not sinned, we make him a liar, and his word is not in us.*

Working out my salvation with fear and trembling (*Philippians 2:12*), knowing that God is not angry nor furious at me all the time; knowing that I will not be doomed to hell if I do not follow the instructions of the cult leader; but learning to adopt a lifestyle in faithful obedient daily living to God's holy Word.

Psalm 119:105
Thy word is a lamp unto my feet, and a light unto my path.

Philippians 3:7-15
7 But what things were gain to me, those I counted loss for Christ.

8 Yea doubtless, and I count all things but loss for the excellency of the knowledge of Christ Jesus my Lord: for whom I have suffered the loss of all things, and do count them but dung, that I may win Christ,

9 And be found in him, not having mine own righteousness, which is of the law, but that which is through the faith of Christ, the righteousness which is of God by faith:

10 That I may know him, and the power of his resurrection, and the fellowship of his sufferings, being made conformable unto his death;

11 If by any means I might attain unto the resurrection of the dead.

12 Not as though I had already attained, either were already perfect: but I follow after, if that I may apprehend that for which also I am apprehended of Christ Jesus.

13 Brethren, I count not myself to have apprehended: but this one thing I do, forgetting those things which are behind, and reaching forth unto those things which are before,

14 I press toward the mark for the prize of the high calling of God in Christ Jesus.

15 Let us therefore, as many as be perfect, be thus minded: and if in any thing ye be otherwise minded, God shall reveal even this unto you

I don't have to be stressed out any longer that my old man "that old woman" as the leader called her, is still there. It is not about destroying her, casting her out and being inhabited by a new spirit which is very demonic. It is all about renewing my inward man day by day as written in the Word of God.

2 Corinthians 4:14-16

14 Knowing that he which raised up the Lord Jesus shall raise up us also by Jesus, and shall present us with you.

15 For all things are for your sakes, that the abundant grace might through the thanksgiving of many redound to the glory of God.

16 For which cause we faint not; but though our outward man perish, yet the inward man is renewed day by day.

Hebrews 12:1b-2

… let us lay aside every weight, and the sin which doth so easily beset us, and let us run with patience the race that is set before us,

2 Looking unto Jesus the author and finisher of our faith; who for the joy that was set before him endured the cross, despising the shame, and is set down at the right hand of the throne of God.

Narcissism

The Holy Spirit began to show me that I had been under the mind control and abuse of an extreme narcissistic religious cult leader. The more I studied about this, the more I began to understand and recognize all the false marks, doctrines and manifestations that I witnessed in the cult.

I went through character assassination, where the leader (the lady) slandered my name publicly which is typical for narcissistic leaders once they lose control over you. Me and some others who stepped away also received the ever recurring letters of threat and judgment. The only way to restore our relationship with God and others, was stepping away from the unhealthy and toxic influence of the leader.

Healing

The path to recovery is not an easy one as it becomes clearer every day how deep the abuse has affected me. Self-care and spending lots of time in God's stillness are essential for my mental health. Strengthening myself in the truth of God's Word is crucial and most important, as Jesus is truly my life saver.

<u>Matthew 6:12, 14-15</u>

12 And forgive us our debts, as we forgive our debtors.

14 For if ye forgive men their trespasses, your heavenly Father will also forgive you:

15 But if ye forgive not men their trespasses, neither will your Father forgive your trespasses.

Finding relief from my own pain is a process, but I chose to forgive the lady because I honour God and I am very thankful as He Himself has forgiven my many sins. I pray that the ones still trapped in the cult may also be set free from deception. I pray that they may see Jesus' Light again, the Way, the Truth and the Life, and that they may turn around from victims to victors.

I give God all the glory and honour for leading me out of the deception and bringing me back home into His eternal arms of love.

> *Galatians 1:8*
>
> *But though we, or an angel from heaven, preach any other gospel unto you than that which we have preached unto you, let him be accursed.*

CHAPTER VII: SALVATION — BE BORN AGAIN

John 3:3

*Jesus answered and said unto him, Verily, verily, I say unto thee, Except a man be **born again**, he cannot see the kingdom of God.*

- o **GOD'S PLAN and will for your salvation**

God is speaking to you today through the Scriptures, where He expresses His infinite love for you, His plan and His will for your Salvation. Every person is born as a sinner and thus we are lost and on our way to hell. It does not matter if you are rich or poor or have accomplished a lot in your life, or even if you do good works every day.

Romans 3:10-12 , 23-25

*[10] As it is written, **There is none righteous**, no, not one:*

[11] There is none that understandeth, there is none that seeketh after God.

[12] They are all gone out of the way, they are together become unprofitable; there is none that doeth good, no, not one.

*[23] **For all have sinned**, and come short of the glory of God;*

[24] Being justified freely by his grace through the redemption that is in Christ Jesus:

[25] Whom God hath set forth to be a propitiation through faith in his blood, to declare his righteousness for the remission of sins that are past, through the forbearance of God;

Acts 16:30-31

*[30] And brought them out, and said, Sirs, **what must I do to be saved?***

³¹ *And they said,* **Believe on the Lord Jesus Christ***, and thou shalt be saved, and thy house.*

o   A GOOD person?

You may think you are a good person, but we all broke God's commandments. How often have you done something that you knew was wrong, but you did it anyway? Have you ever lied, stolen, cheated, cursed, fornicated, or worshiped other gods? Have you ever wanted or desired something that belongs to someone else? Have you ever looked at someone (*outside of your marriage*) with lust? Perhaps you still hold unforgiveness in your heart? **So you're a sinner.** Our heart is deceitful above all things.

Jeremiah 17:9-10

⁹ *The heart is* **deceitful** *above all things, and desperately* **wicked***: who can know it?*

¹⁰ *I the* LORD *search the heart, I try the reins, even to give every man according to his ways, and according to the fruit of his doings.*

o   JUDGMENT SEAT of Christ

We will all stand before the judgment seat of Christ one day. He is just and we will have to give an account of every thought, word and deed, whether it is good or bad. We will all be found guilty on the Day of Judgment. Though our conscience has shown us right from wrong, it does not matter, we will be without excuse. God will give us justice, and hell will be the place of our eternal punishment.

Romans 14:10

But why dost thou judge thy brother? or why dost thou set at nought thy brother? for we shall all stand before the **judgment seat of Christ***.*

Matthew 10:26

*Fear them not **therefore**: for **there is nothing covered**, that shall not be revealed; and hid, that shall not be known.*

- ○ **BUT GOD is rich in mercy to all that call upon Him**

Ephesians 2:4-9

*[4] But God, **who is rich in mercy**, for his great love wherewith he loved us,*

[5] Even when we were dead in sins, hath quickened us together with Christ, (by grace ye are saved;)

[6] And hath raised us up together, and made us sit together in heavenly places in Christ Jesus:

[7] That in the ages to come he might shew the exceeding riches of his grace in his kindness toward us through Christ Jesus.

[8] For by grace are ye saved through faith; and that not of yourselves: it is the gift of God:

[9] Not of works, lest any man should boast.

God sent Jesus Christ to earth to rescue us from the consequence of our sin and to reconcile us with God, through the work of Jesus Christ on the cross.

John 3:16-17

*[16] For God so **loved** the world, that he gave **his only begotten Son**, that whosoever believeth in him should not perish, but have everlasting life.*

[17] For God sent not his Son into the world to condemn the world; but that the world through him might be saved.

John 24: 5

*Verily, verily, I say unto you, He that **heareth** my word, and **believeth on him** that sent me, hath **everlasting life**, and shall **not** come into condemnation; but is passed from death unto life.*

- o **JESUS PAID the price for us**

Jesus bore the full penalty of our sins. He was resurrected and broke the power of death over sin and defeated satan and all principalities and powers.

Colossians 2:12-15

[12] ***Buried** with him in **baptism**, wherein also ye are **risen** with him through the faith of the operation of God, who hath **raised** him from the dead.*

[13] *And you, being dead in your sins and the uncircumcision of your flesh, hath he quickened together with him, having forgiven you all trespasses;*

[14] *Blotting out the handwriting of ordinances that was against us, which was contrary to us, and took it out of the way, nailing it to his cross;*

[15] *And having spoiled principalities and powers, he made a shew of them openly, triumphing over them in it.*

Romans 6:20-23

[20] *For when ye were the **servants of sin**, ye were free from righteousness.*

[21] *What fruit had ye then in those things whereof ye are now ashamed? for the end of those things is death.*

[22] *But now being made free from sin, and become servants to God, ye have your fruit unto holiness, and the end everlasting life.*

23 *For the wages of sin is death; but the gift of God is eternal life through Jesus Christ our Lord.*

- o **SALVATION ONLY in Jesus Christ**

Salvation is found in no one else, for there is no other name given under Heaven by which we must be saved.

Acts 4:12
*Neither is there salvation in any other: **for there is none other name under heaven** given among men, whereby we must be saved.*

Romans 5: 8-10
*8 But God commendeth his love toward us, in that, while we were yet **sinners, Christ died for us**.*

9 Much more then, being now justified by his blood, we shall be saved from wrath through him.

10 For if, when we were enemies, we were reconciled to God by the death of his Son, much more, being reconciled, we shall be saved by his life.

Romans 10:8-11
*8 But what saith it? The word is nigh thee, even in **thy mouth**, and in **thy heart**: that is, the word of faith, which we preach;*

*9 That if thou shalt **confess with thy mouth** the Lord Jesus, and shalt **believe in thine heart** that God hath raised him from the dead, thou shalt be saved.*

10 For with the heart man believeth unto righteousness; and with the mouth confession is made unto salvation.

11 For the scripture saith, Whosoever believeth on him shall not be ashamed.

- ○ **INVITE JESUS today**

If you do not have a relationship with the Lord Jesus Christ yet, you can do this today. Heaven and hell are real. Eternal death and Eternal Life are real. If you would die today, where will you spend eternity?

Luke 16:22-26

22 *And it came to pass, that the beggar **died**, and was carried by the angels into **Abraham's bosom**: the rich man also died, and was buried;*

23 *And **in hell** he lift up his eyes, being **in torments**, and seeth Abraham afar off, and Lazarus in his bosom.*

24 *And he cried and said, Father Abraham, have mercy on me, and send Lazarus, that he may dip the tip of his finger in water, and cool my tongue; for I am tormented in this flame.*

25 *But Abraham said, Son, remember that thou in thy lifetime receivedst thy good things, and likewise Lazarus evil things: but now he is comforted, and thou art tormented.*

26 *And beside all this, between us and you there is a great gulf fixed: so that they which would pass from hence to you cannot; neither can they pass to us, that would come from thence.*

Matthew 25:46

46 *And these shall go away into everlasting punishment: but the righteous into life eternal.*

Today is the day for your salvation. Please call on the Lord Jesus Christ, repent of your sin and accept Him as your Saviour and Lord over your life. Honour Christ's command to be baptized and get a Bible to feed on the Word of God.
May God continue to bless you as you grow in your faith.

Acts 2:38

*Then Peter said unto them, **Repent**, and be **baptized** every one of you in the name of Jesus Christ for the remission of sins, and ye shall receive the gift of **the Holy Ghost**.*

Mark 16:16

He that believeth and is baptized shall be saved; but he that believeth not shall be damned.

Matthew 11:28-30

*28 Come unto me, all ye that labour and are heavy laden, and I will give you **rest**.*

29 Take my yoke upon you, and learn of me; for I am meek and lowly in heart: and ye shall find rest unto your souls.

30 For my yoke is easy, and my burden is light.

Galatians 5:22-25

*22 But **the fruit of the Spirit** is love, joy, peace, longsuffering, gentleness, goodness, faith,*

23 Meekness, temperance: against such there is no law.

24 And they that are Christ's have crucified the flesh with the affections and lusts.

25 If we live in the Spirit, let us also walk in the Spirit.

Related Scriptures

Genesis 2:18 *And the LORD God said, It is not good that the man should be alone; I will make him an help meet for him.*

Exodus 20:16 *Thou shalt not bear false witness against thy neighbour.*

Leviticus 18:22 *Thou shalt not lie with mankind, as with womankind: it is abomination.*

Leviticus 19:31 *Regard not them that have familiar spirits, neither seek after wizards, to be defiled by them: I am the LORD your God.*

Deuteronomy 18:20-22 *But the prophet, which shall presume to speak a word in my name, which I have not commanded him to speak, or that shall speak in the name of other gods, even that prophet shall die. 21 And if thou say in thine heart, How shall we know the word which the LORD hath not spoken? 22 When a prophet speaketh in the name of the LORD, if the thing follow not, nor come to pass, that is the thing which the LORD hath not spoken, but the prophet hath spoken it presumptuously: thou shalt not be afraid of him.*

1 Chronicles 10:13-14 *So Saul died for his transgression which he committed against the LORD, even against the word of the LORD, which he kept not, and also for asking counsel of one that had a familiar spirit, to enquire of it; 14 And enquired not of the LORD: therefore he slew him, and turned the kingdom unto David the son of Jesse.*

Psalm 138:2 *I will worship toward thy holy temple, and praise thy name for thy lovingkindness and for thy truth: for thou hast magnified thy word above all thy name.*

Isaiah 8:19 *And when they shall say unto you, Seek unto them that have familiar spirits, and unto wizards that peep, and that mutter: should not a people seek unto their God? for the living to the dead?*

Matthew 5:13-16 *Ye are the salt of the earth: but if the salt have lost his savour, wherewith shall it be salted? it is thenceforth good for nothing, but to be cast out, and to be trodden under foot of men. 14 Ye are the light of the world. A city that is set on an hill cannot be hid. 15 Neither do men light a candle, and put it under a bushel, but on a candlestick; and it giveth light unto all that are in the house. 16 Let your light so shine before men, that they may see your good works, and glorify your Father which is in heaven.*

Matthew 5:17-22 *Think not that I am come to destroy the law, or the prophets: I am not come to destroy, but to fulfil. 18 For verily I say unto you, Till heaven and earth pass, one jot or one tittle shall in no wise pass from the law, till all be fulfilled. 19 Whosoever therefore shall break one of these least commandments, and shall teach men so, he shall be called the least in the kingdom of heaven: but whosoever shall do and teach them, the same shall be called great in the kingdom of heaven. 20 For I say unto you, That except your righteousness shall exceed the righteousness of the scribes and Pharisees, ye shall in no case enter into the kingdom of heaven. 21 Ye have heard that it was said of them of old time, Thou shalt not kill; and whosoever shall kill shall be in danger of the judgment: 22 But I say unto you, That whosoever is angry with his brother without a cause shall be in danger of the judgment: and whosoever shall say to his brother, Raca, shall be in danger of the council: but whosoever shall say, Thou fool, shall be in danger of hell fire.*

Matthew 19:6 *Wherefore they are no more twain, but one flesh. What therefore God hath joined together, let not man put asunder.*

Matthew 19:16-23 *And, behold, one came and said unto him, Good Master, what good thing shall I do, that I may have eternal life?*

17 And he said unto him, Why callest thou me good? there is none good but one, that is, God: but if thou wilt enter into life, keep the commandments. 18 He saith unto him, Which? Jesus said, Thou shalt do no murder, Thou shalt not commit adultery, Thou shalt not steal, Thou shalt not bear false witness, 19 Honour thy father and thy mother: and, Thou shalt love thy neighbour as thyself. 20 The young man saith unto him, All these things have I kept from my youth up: what lack I yet? 21 Jesus said unto him, If thou wilt be perfect, go and sell that thou hast, and give to the poor, and thou shalt have treasure in heaven: and come and follow me. 22 But when the young man heard that saying, he went away sorrowful: for he had great possessions. 23 Then said Jesus unto his disciples, Verily I say unto you, That a rich man shall hardly enter into the kingdom of heaven.

Matthew 24:4-5; 23-26 *And Jesus answered and said unto them, Take heed that no man deceive you. 5 For many shall come in my name, saying, I am Christ; and shall deceive many. 23 Then if any man shall say unto you, Lo, here is Christ, or there; believe it not. 24 For there shall arise false Christs, and false prophets, and shall shew great signs and wonders; insomuch that, if it were possible, they shall deceive the very elect. 25 Behold, I have told you before. 26 Wherefore if they shall say unto you, Behold, he is in the desert; go not forth: behold, he is in the secret chambers; believe it not.*

Matthew 28:19 *Go ye therefore, and teach all nations, baptizing them in the name of the Father, and of the Son, and of the Holy Ghost:*

Luke 10:27-28 *And he answering said, Thou shalt love the Lord thy God with all thy heart, and with all thy soul, and with all thy strength, and with all thy mind; and thy neighbour as thyself. 28 And he said unto him, Thou hast answered right: this do, and thou shalt live.*

Luke 10:30-37 *And Jesus answering said, A certain man went down from Jerusalem to Jericho, and fell among thieves, which stripped him* *of his raiment, and wounded him, and departed, leaving him half dead. 31 And by chance there came down a certain priest that way: and when he saw him, he passed by on the other side. 32 And likewise a Levite, when he was at the place, came and looked on him, and passed by on the other side. 33 But a certain Samaritan, as he journeyed, came where he was: and when he saw him, he had compassion on him, 34 And went to him, and bound up his wounds, pouring in oil and wine, and set him on his own beast, and brought him to an inn, and took care of him. 35 And on the morrow when he departed, he took out two pence, and gave them to the host, and said unto him, Take care of him; and whatsoever thou spendest more, when I come again, I will repay thee. 36 Which now of these three, thinkest thou, was neighbour unto him that fell among the thieves? 37 And he said, He that shewed mercy on him. Then said Jesus unto him, Go, and do thou likewise.*

John 3:16 *For God so loved the world, that he gave his only begotten Son, that whosoever believeth in him should not perish, but have everlasting life.*

John 8:31-32 *Then said Jesus to those Jews which believed on him, If ye continue in my word, then are ye my disciples indeed; 32 And ye shall know the truth, and the truth shall make you free.*

John 8:44 *Ye are of your father the devil, and the lusts of your father ye will do. He was a murderer from the beginning, and abode not in the truth, because there is no truth in him. When he speaketh a lie, he speaketh of his own: for he is a liar, and the father of it.*

Romans 8:9-11 *But ye are not in the flesh, but in the Spirit, if so be that the Spirit of God dwell in you. Now if any man have not the Spirit of Christ, he is none of his. 10 And if Christ be in you, the body is dead because of sin; but the Spirit is life because of righteousness. 11 But if the Spirit of him that raised up Jesus from the dead dwell in you, he that raised up Christ from the dead shall also quicken your mortal bodies by his Spirit that dwelleth in you.*

Romans 8:13-17; 38-39 *For if ye live after the flesh, ye shall die: but if ye through the Spirit do mortify the deeds of the body, ye shall live. 14 For as many as are led by the Spirit of God, they are the sons of God. 15 For ye have not received the spirit of bondage again to fear; but ye have received the Spirit of adoption, whereby we cry, Abba, Father. 16 The Spirit itself beareth witness with our spirit, that we are the children of God: 17 And if children, then heirs; heirs of God, and joint-heirs with Christ; if so be that we suffer with him, that we may be also glorified together. 38 For I am persuaded, that neither death, nor life, nor angels, nor principalities, nor powers, nor things present, nor things to come, 39 Nor height, nor depth, nor any other creature, shall be able to separate us from the love of God, which is in Christ Jesus our Lord.*

John 8:51 *Verily, verily, I say unto you, If a man keep my saying, he shall never see death.*

1 Corinthians 5:6 *Your glorying is not good. Know ye not that a little leaven leaveneth the whole lump?*

1 Corinthians 7:3-5 *Let the husband render unto the wife due benevolence: and likewise also the wife unto the husband. 4 The wife hath not power of her own body, but the husband: and likewise also the husband hath not power of his own body, but the wife. 5 Defraud ye not one the other, except it be with consent for a time, that ye may give yourselves to fasting and prayer; and come together again, that Satan tempt you not for your incontinency.*

1 Corinthians 7:10 *And unto the married I command, yet not I, but the Lord, Let not the wife depart from her husband:*

1 Corinthians 15:33-34 *Be not deceived: evil communications corrupt good manners. 34 Awake to righteousness, and sin not; for some have not the knowledge of God: I speak this to your shame.*

2 Corinthians 3:17-18 *Now the Lord is that Spirit: and where the Spirit of the Lord is, there is liberty.* [18] *But we all, with open face beholding as in a glass the glory of the Lord, are changed into the same image from glory to glory, even as by the Spirit of the Lord.*

2 Corinthians 4:2 *But have renounced the hidden things of dishonesty, not walking in craftiness, nor handling the word of God deceitfully; but by manifestation of the truth commending ourselves to every man's conscience in the sight of God.*

2 Corinthians 9:6-7 *But this I say, He which soweth sparingly shall reap also sparingly; and he which soweth bountifully shall reap also bountifully. 7 Every man according as he purposeth in his heart, so let him give; not grudgingly, or of necessity: for God loveth a cheerful giver.*

2 Corinthians 11:13-15 *For such are false apostles, deceitful workers, transforming themselves into the apostles of Christ. 14 And no marvel; for Satan himself is transformed into an angel of light. 15 Therefore it is no great thing if his ministers also be transformed as the ministers of righteousness; whose end shall be according to their works.*

Galatians 5: 20-21 *Idolatry, witchcraft, hatred, variance, emulations, wrath, strife, seditions, heresies, 21 Envyings, murders, drunkenness, revellings, and such like: of the which I tell you before, as I have also told you in time past, that they which do such things shall not inherit the kingdom of God.*

Ephesians 4:25 *Wherefore putting away lying, speak every man truth with his neighbour: for we are members one of another.*

Ephesians 4:29-32 *Let no corrupt communication proceed out of your mouth, but that which is good to the use of edifying, that it may minister grace unto the hearers. 30 And grieve not the holy Spirit of*

God, whereby ye are sealed unto the day of redemption. 31 Let all bitterness, and wrath, and anger, and clamour, and evil speaking, be put away from you, with all malice: 32 And be ye kind one to another, tenderhearted, forgiving one another, even as God for Christ's sake hath forgiven you.

Ephesians 5:21-33 *Submitting yourselves one to another in the fear of God. 22 Wives, submit yourselves unto your own husbands, as unto the Lord. 23 For the husband is the head of the wife, even as Christ is the head of the church: and he is the saviour of the body. 24 Therefore as the church is subject unto Christ, so let the wives be to their own husbands in every thing. 25 Husbands, love your wives, even as Christ also loved the church, and gave himself for it; 26 That he might sanctify and cleanse it with the washing of water by the word, 27 That he might present it to himself a glorious church, not having spot, or wrinkle, or any such thing; but that it should be holy and without blemish. 28 So ought men to love their wives as their own bodies. He that loveth his wife loveth himself. 29 For no man ever yet hated his own flesh; but nourisheth and cherisheth it, even as the Lord the church: 30 For we are members of his body, of his flesh, and of his bones. 31 For this cause shall a man leave his father and mother, and shall be joined unto his wife, and they two shall be one flesh. 32 This is a great mystery: but I speak concerning Christ and the church. 33 Nevertheless let every one of you in particular so love his wife even as himself; and the wife see that she reverence her husband.*

Colossians 1:23 *If ye continue in the faith grounded and settled, and be not moved away from the hope of the gospel, which ye have heard, and which was preached to every creature which is under heaven; whereof I Paul am made a minister.*

Colossians 2:20-23 *Wherefore if ye be dead with Christ from the rudiments of the world, why, as though living in the world, are ye subject to ordinances, 21 (Touch not; taste not; handle not; 22 Which all are to perish with the using;) after the commandments and* doctrines of men? 23 Which things have indeed a shew of wisdom in will worship, and humility, and neglecting of the body: not in any honour to the satisfying of the flesh.

2 Thessalonians 3:16 *Now the Lord of peace himself give you peace always by all means. The Lord be with you all. 5 For it is sanctified by the word of God and prayer.*

1 Timothy 4:1-4 *Now the Spirit speaketh expressly, that in the latter times some shall depart from the faith, giving heed to seducing spirits, and doctrines of devils; 2 Speaking lies in hypocrisy; having their conscience seared with a hot iron; 3 Forbidding to marry, and commanding to abstain from meats, which God hath created to be received with thanksgiving of them which believe and know the truth. 4 For every creature of God is good, and nothing to be refused, if it be received with thanksgiving:*

2 Timothy 3:2-5 *This know also, that in the last days perilous times shall come. 2 For men shall be lovers of their own selves, covetous, boasters, proud, blasphemers, disobedient to parents, unthankful, unholy, 3 Without natural affection, trucebreakers, false accusers, incontinent, fierce, despisers of those that are good, 4 Traitors, heady, highminded, lovers of pleasures more than lovers of God; 5 Having a form of godliness, but denying the power thereof: from such turn away.*

2 Timothy 4:5 *But watch thou in all things, endure afflictions, do the work of an evangelist, make full proof of thy ministry.*

James 2:8-14 *If ye fulfil the royal law according to the scripture, Thou shalt love thy neighbour as thyself, ye do well: 9 But if ye have respect to persons, ye commit sin, and are convinced of the law as transgressors. 10 For whosoever shall keep the whole law, and yet offend in one point, he is guilty of all. 11 For he that said, Do not commit adultery, said also, Do not kill. Now if thou commit no* *adultery, yet if thou kill, thou art become a transgressor of the law. 12 So speak ye, and so do, as they that shall be judged by the law of liberty. 13 For he shall have judgment without mercy, that hath shewed no mercy; and mercy rejoiceth against judgment. 14 What doth it profit, my brethren, though a man say he hath faith, and have not works? can faith save him?*

James 4:4 *Ye adulterers and adulteresses, know ye not that the friendship of the world is enmity with God? whosoever therefore will be a friend of the world is the enemy of God.*

1 Peter 3:1-8 *Likewise, ye wives, be in subjection to your own husbands; that, if any obey not the word, they also may without the word be won by the conversation of the wives; 2 While they behold your chaste conversation coupled with fear. 3 Whose adorning let it not be that outward adorning of plaiting the hair, and of wearing of gold, or of putting on of apparel; 4 But let it be the hidden man of the heart, in that which is not corruptible, even the ornament of a meek and quiet spirit, which is in the sight of God of great price. 5 For after this manner in the old time the holy women also, who trusted in God, adorned themselves, being in subjection unto their own husbands: 6 Even as Sara obeyed Abraham, calling him lord: whose daughters ye are, as long as ye do well, and are not afraid with any amazement. 7 Likewise, ye husbands, dwell with them according to knowledge, giving honour unto the wife, as unto the weaker vessel, and as being heirs together of the grace of life; that your prayers be not hindered. 8 Finally, be ye all of one mind, having compassion one of another, love as brethren, be pitiful, be courteous:*

2 Peter 2:1-22 *But there were false prophets also among the people, even as there shall be false teachers among you, who privily shall bring in damnable heresies, even denying the Lord that bought them, and bring upon themselves swift destruction. 2 And many shall follow their pernicious ways; by reason of whom the way of truth shall be evil spoken of. 4 For if God spared not the angels that sinned, but cast* *them down to hell, and delivered them into chains of darkness, to be reserved unto judgment; 5 And spared not the old world, but saved Noah the eighth person, a preacher of righteousness, bringing in the flood upon the world of the ungodly; 6 And turning the cities of Sodom and Gomorrha into ashes condemned them with an overthrow, making them an ensample unto those that after should live ungodly; 7 And delivered just Lot, vexed with the filthy conversation of the wicked: 8 (For that righteous man dwelling among them, in seeing and hearing, vexed his righteous soul from day to day with their unlawful deeds;) 9 The Lord knoweth how to deliver the godly out of temptations, and to reserve the unjust unto the day of judgment to be punished: 10 But chiefly them that walk after the flesh in the lust of uncleanness, and despise government. Presumptuous are they, selfwilled, they are not afraid to speak evil of dignities. 11 Whereas angels, which are greater in power and might, bring not railing accusation against them before the Lord. 12 But these, as natural brute beasts, made to be taken and destroyed, speak evil of the things that they understand not; and shall utterly perish in their own corruption; 13 And shall receive the reward of unrighteousness, as they that count it pleasure to riot in the day time. Spots they are and blemishes, sporting themselves with their own deceivings while they feast with you; 14 Having eyes full of adultery, and that cannot cease from sin; beguiling unstable souls: an heart they have exercised with covetous practices; cursed children: 15 Which have forsaken the right way, and are gone astray, following the way of Balaam the son of Bosor, who loved the wages of unrighteousness; 16 But was rebuked for his iniquity: the dumb ass speaking with man's voice forbad the madness of the prophet. 17 These are wells without water, clouds that are carried with a tempest; to whom the mist of darkness is reserved for ever. 18 For when they speak great swelling words of vanity, they allure through the lusts of the flesh, through much wantonness, those that were clean escaped from them who live in error. 19 While they promise them liberty, they themselves are the servants of corruption: for of whom a man is overcome, of the same is he brought in bondage. 20 For if after they have escaped the pollutions of the world through* the knowledge of the Lord and Saviour Jesus Christ, they are again entangled therein, and overcome, the latter end is worse with them than the beginning. 21 For it had been better for them not to have known the way of righteousness, than, after they have known it, to turn from the holy commandment delivered unto them. 22 But it is happened unto them according to the true proverb, The dog is turned to his own vomit again; and the sow that was washed to her wallowing in the mire.

1 John 2:3-6 *And hereby we do know that we know him, if we keep his commandments. 4 He that saith, I know him, and keepeth not his commandments, is a liar, and the truth is not in him. 5 But whoso keepeth his word, in him verily is the love of God perfected: hereby know we that we are in him. 6 He that saith he abideth in him ought himself also so to walk, even as he walked.*

1 John 3:10-11 *In this the children of God are manifest, and the children of the devil: whosoever doeth not righteousness is not of God, neither he that loveth not his brother. 11 For this is the message that ye heard from the beginning, that we should love one another.*

1 John 3:14-18 *We know that we have passed from death unto life, because we love the brethren. He that loveth not his brother abideth in death. 15 Whosoever hateth his brother is a murderer: and ye know that no murderer hath eternal life abiding in him. 16 Hereby perceive we the love of God, because he laid down his life for us: and we ought to lay down our lives for the brethren. 17 But whoso hath this world's good, and seeth his brother have need, and shutteth up his bowels of compassion from him, how dwelleth the love of God in him? 18 My little children, let us not love in word, neither in tongue; but in deed and in truth.*

1 John 3:22-24 *And whatsoever we ask, we receive of him, because we keep his commandments, and do those things that are pleasing in his sight. 23 And this is his commandment, That we should believe on the* name of his Son Jesus Christ, and love one another, as he gave us commandment. 24 And he that keepeth his commandments dwelleth in him, and he in him. And hereby we know that he abideth in us, by the Spirit which he hath given us.

1 John 4:1 Beloved, believe not every spirit, but try the spirits whether they are of God: because many false prophets are gone out into the world.

1 John 4:10-12 Herein is love, not that we loved God, but that he loved us, and sent his Son to be the propitiation for our sins. 11 Beloved, if God so loved us, we ought also to love one another. 12 No man hath seen God at any time. If we love one another, God dwelleth in us, and his love is perfected in us.

1 John 4:18 There is no fear in love; but perfect love casteth out fear: because fear hath torment. He that feareth is not made perfect in love.

Revelation 19:6 And I heard as it were the voice of a great multitude, and as the voice of many waters, and as the voice of mighty thunderings, saying, Alleluia: for the Lord God omnipotent reigneth.

Revelation 21:8 But the fearful, and unbelieving, and the abominable, and murderers, and whoremongers, and sorcerers, and idolaters, and all liars, shall have their part in the lake which burneth with fire and brimstone: which is the second death.

Revelation 22:13 I am Alpha and Omega, the beginning and the end, the first and the last.

Revelation 22:15 For without are dogs, and sorcerers, and whoremongers, and murderers, and idolaters, and whosoever loveth and maketh a lie.

–Revelation 22:18 –
For I testify unto every man that heareth the
words of the prophecy of this book,
If any man shall add unto these things,
God shall add unto him the plagues that are
written in this book:

And if any man shall take away
from the words of the book of this prophecy,
God shall take away his part
out of the book of life, and out of the holy city,
and from the things
which are written in this book.

Endnote

At this present time, August 2021, my husband is still not back yet. Every day I cry out to my Heavenly Father for him to return. I believe God will show him His truth and that he will be back one day. A lot of emotional and spiritual healing comes forth during this time.

Every day God's amazing Love, Hope, Grace and Mercy are healing my heart a little bit more. I love to spend time in His Word. The peaceful silence is filled with His tangible Presence. The lush green and the variety of the multitude of flowers in the little garden, witness every day what a beautiful creative God He is. The young sparrows playing around and chasing the insects on the grapevine, are putting a smile on my face. My beautiful pet chickens are all special gifts from my heavenly Father. God is good and He cares for you, for me and for the little sparrows.

*"Are not two sparrows sold for a farthing? and one of them shall not
fall on the ground without your Father.
But the very hairs of your head are all numbered.
Fear ye not therefore,
ye are of more value than many sparrows."*
–Matthew 10: 29-31–

Since 2011, God led me through a nine-year wilderness journey. His protecting Hand was always over me, He kept me safe, He never left me and literally saved my life many times. I thought I lost it all, but then He said:

"You are not losing anything—you are gaining everything."

Only now I truly understand the depth of these amazing words. Eternal Life is the most precious gift.

Maybe you are in a place right now where you lost all your hope; maybe you have no more strength to continue on and you just want to give up?

Hope in God's Mercy, He is saying to you today:

"Come unto me, all ye that labour and are heavy laden,
and I will give you rest.
Take my yoke upon you, and learn of me;
for I am meek and lowly in heart:
and ye shall find rest unto your souls."
–Matthew 11:28-29–

God is reaching out to you. Jesus is the only Truth and He wants to set you free. Call upon Him now. Psalm 86:5: *For thou, Lord, art good, and ready to forgive; and plenteous in mercy unto all them that call upon thee.*

May God fill you with all His Hope.
May He touch you with His Grace.
May He embrace you with His Mercy.
May His precious Gift of eternal life be yours today.

"The LORD bless thee, and keep thee:

The LORD make his face shine upon thee,
and be gracious unto thee:

The LORD lift up his countenance upon thee,
and give thee peace."
–Numbers 6: 24-26–

–Psalm 57:7-11–

7 *My heart is fixed, O God, my heart is fixed:*
I will sing and give praise.

8 *Awake up, my glory; awake, psaltery and harp:*
I myself will awake early.

9 *I will praise thee, O Lord, among the people:*
I will sing unto thee among the nations.

10 *For thy mercy is great unto the heavens,*
and thy truth unto the clouds.

11 *Be thou exalted, O God, above the heavens:*
let thy glory be above all the earth.

~ ~ ~

Other book

Why are you persecuting Me?

What if you are deceived but you do not know that you are deceived? What if you are in a Cult, but you do not know you are in a Cult.

How do abusive religious leaders operate? In this book I will list and describe the actual mind control tactics that I went through in the religious cult. The focus was on one woman claiming to be the one and only bride of Christ, the birth of a physical holy man child, the preparation of the 144,000 and the coming of Christ in the flesh to birth this man child.

These cult leaders may be very intelligent, well educated and have an outstanding ability to charm, seduce, influence and control you with their mind control and "gaslighting" brainwashing techniques They indoctrinate you with new things and repeat them often enough until you eventually believe it. They camouflage themselves in their Biblical knowledge and prophesy over you, then bombard you with all the mysteries and oracles from heaven. This makes it not so easy to discern that they are actually deceiving you, while they may exhibit behavioural characteristics or signs of extremism, narcissism, even sociopathic tendancies.

My husband left me this note one day:

FOR I KNOW
THE PLANS
I HAVE FOR
~YOU~
DECLARES
THE LORD

Plans to prosper you
And not to harm you
Plans to give you HOPE
And a future.

Jeremiah 29:11

Printed in Great Britain
by Amazon

64974558R00147